PARTY FARE
Irresistible Nibbles for Every Occasion

Joanna White

BRISTOL PUBLISHING ENTERPRISES
San Leandro, California

a nitty gritty® cookbook

Printed in the United States of America.

ISBN 1-55867-218-4

Material previously published as **Appetizers** ©1996 Bristol Publishing Enterprises, Inc.

Cover design: Frank J. Paredes
Cover photography: John A. Benson
Food styling: Susan Massey
Illustrations: James Balkovek

CONTENTS

TIPS FOR SERVING PARTY FARE

Appetizers, hors d'oeuvres, starters, nibbles or small plates — call them what you will. These dishes are not the main course, but tempting tidbits that should excite rather than satiate the appetite.

- If serving predinner appetizers, the cardinal rule should be: keep it light.
- If serving a "starter," an appetizer eaten at the table before dinner is served, be certain that the dish complements the rest of the meal you are serving.
- If serving hors d'oeuvres for a cocktail party or buffet, a variety of selections in a substantial amount is the ruling guide.
- If serving several small dishes at once, be certain that they complement one another. It is important to balance flavors and textures, hot and cold, raw and cooked, simple and elegant.

Overall, one of the most important rules is: choose your party fare so that you can enjoy time with your guests and not be tied to the kitchen. Planning is the key to a successful party.

PARTY FARE GUIDELINES

- Serve a contrast of hot and cold dishes.
- Offer different textures for food served together, such as crisp vegetables or crackers with a creamy dip.
- Avoid being monotonous with flavor — for example, using onions in every recipe.
- Think variety: plan on serving dishes with different ingredients and textures.
- When serving hors d'oeuvres on trays, supplement with self-help foods like spreads and patés.
- If possible, disperse food stations throughout the room to encourage socializing.
- When serving a buffet, serve some dishes that add height to the presentation. Make sure hot foods are accessible.
- Coordinate appetizers with the type of cuisine being served for dinner, such as dim sum before a Chinese meal, or tapas before Spanish cuisine.
- To prevent soggy tea sandwiches and canapés, spread softened butter or cream cheese over the bread before applying the filling. Calculate about ¼ lb. butter or cream cheese for every loaf of bread.

- If guests are standing and holding a glass in one hand, consider serving only finger foods so they won't have to do a balancing act.
- If appetizers are replacing dinner, count on 10 to 12 "bites" per person, and offer at least 5 to 6 choices.
- A general rule for quantity at cocktail parties is to consider at least 6 appetizers per person per hour.

A PANTRY FULL OF PARTY FARE

Prepared foods in jars, bottles, cans and packages can provide instant, delicious party fare for drop-in guests. A well-stocked pantry is the harried host's best friend.

anchovies: mash and mix with oil, butter or cream cheese for spreads

artichokes: marinated or plain; serve on an antipasto platter, or mix with cream cheese for spreads

crusty or flavored breads: to dip and spread

capers: sprinkle on top of creamy spreads for piquant flavor

caviar: serve as a decorative garnish on many items, to those who appreciate it

cheeses: hard cheeses to shred and sprinkle over fillings on toasted bread; soft cheeses to serve with crackers or to make spreads

chips: a variety of potato chips, corn chips and bagel chips for dippers

chutney: add flavor to dips and spreads

corn tortillas: fry or bake into chips or make small filled tortillas from leftovers

crackers: an assortment to serve with dips and cheeses

deviled spreads: ham, chicken or beef, to spread on bread rounds or crackers

eggs: add chopped hard cooked eggs to mayonnaise for spreads

fish: smoked or not, canned or frozen; serve on an antipasto platter or mix into spreads

green chiles: diced; mix into spreads or sprinkle on cheese dishes

ham: canned; cut into chunks for dippers or add to spreads

horseradish: add heat to sauces, dips and spreads

mayonnaise: a quick, essential base for spreads

meats: a variety of sliced luncheon meats for an antipasto platter

mustards: a variety to make sauces, dips and to serve on breads

nuts: a variety to serve as is or to flavor with butter, sugar and/or spices

oils: a variety of flavors for frying, creating dips or spreading on bread

olives: a variety for serving as is; or chop and add to spreads

onions: cocktail; serve on an antipasto platter

patés: canned or from the deli case to spread on crusty bread, toast or crackers

patés: canned or from the deli case to spread on crusty bread, toast or crackers

pepper jelly: serve over cream cheese with crackers

peppers: bottled pickled peppers to serve on an antipasto platter

pesto: mix with cream cheese for spreads

pickles: serve whole or chop and add to spreads and dips

pie crust: make pastry shells by lining miniature or regular muffin tins or tart tins and baking at 350° until brown; fill immediately or freeze

pita bread: to dip; or to butter, sprinkle with herbs and bake

puff pastry: make pastry shells by follow instructions for pie crust, but prick pastry several times with a fork before baking

sandwich bread: make toast cups by trimming crust from bread, brushing both sides with melted butter and pressing slices carefully into muffin tins to form cups with 4 uniform points; toast in a 350° oven until crisp and golden brown

sun-dried tomatoes: serve on top of or mix into bread spreads

vegetables: cut-up in bags or bottled, marinated; use as dippers or part of an antipasto platter

vinegars: a variety of flavored vinegars for sauces and dips

water chestnuts: add crunch to dips and spreads

STORING PARTY FARE

- Store all foods in tightly covered containers to prevent drying.
- Use airtight containers if planning on freezing foods.
- Freeze foods in a single layer on a baking sheet. Then, stack frozen foods between layers of waxed paper.
- If using bags for freezing, use only moisture/vapor-proof freezer bags.
- Glass containers with airtight lids are acceptable storage containers for appetizers.
- Tea sandwiches can be frozen as long as the filling ingredients can be frozen. Fillings made with butter or cream cheese are ideal for freezing.
- Do not freeze lettuce, fresh vegetables, tomatoes, eggs, mayonnaise, salad dressings, aspics or mousses.
- Freeze baked pastry shells and toast cups separate from their filling in airtight containers. Before serving, bake in a 350° oven for 10 to 15 minutes before adding filling.

FLAVORED NIBBLERS

MARINATED OLIVES

This recipe gives American olives a Greek flavor. It also makes a great gift to give friends for the holidays.

1 lb. large black olives, pitted or
   unpitted
3 stalks celery, finely chopped
3-4 cloves garlic, minced
juice of 2 lemons

1 whole lemon, cut into small pieces
1 cup extra virgin olive oil
1½ cups balsamic or red wine vinegar
2 tbs. dried oregano

Sterilize 2 pint canning jars by submerging them in boiling water for 15 minutes; remove jars and air-dry. Submerge lids in boiling water for 3 minutes; remove and air-dry.

Drain olives and, if unpitted, slit one side with a knife to allow marinade to penetrate. Mix remaining ingredients with olives in a bowl. Pack mixture into sterilized jars, making sure liquid completely covers olives. Add a little water if necessary. Clear jar tops well and seal with sterilized lids. Let stand 2 to 3 weeks in a cool, dark place, shaking jars every few days. Serve with toothpicks and small containers for olive pits, if necessary. Provide toothpicks for serving.

MARINATED VEGETABLES

Consider an artful display of marinated vegetables instead of the standard vegetable tray. For additional color and flavor, add a variety of black and green olives. Alternative vegetables can be substituted, such as tomatoes and mushrooms.

1 head broccoli
1 head cauliflower
4-5 carrots
2 cloves garlic, minced
1½ cups balsamic vinegar
2½ cups extra virgin olive oil
1½ tbs. dried dill weed
1½ tbs. sugar
1½ tsp. salt
1½ tsp. pepper

Cut broccoli and cauliflower tops into bite-sized florets. Peel broccoli stems and cut stems into thin slices on the diagonal. Peel carrots and cut into diagonal slices. Place vegetables in a bowl. Process remaining ingredients with a food processor or blender until well mixed. Taste and adjust seasonings. Pour mixture over vegetables in bowl, cover and refrigerate overnight. Provide toothpicks for serving.

VEGETABLE ANTIPASTO (GIARDINIERA)

Make a large batch of this when the vegetables are at their peak to keep in the refrigerator year-round. Serve this on a platter with a few fresh vegetables, such as green onions, and perhaps some slices of good salami.

8 carrots, peeled and cut into 3-inch sticks
8 stalks celery, cut into 3-inch sticks
2 small zucchini, cut into 3-inch sticks
2 red bell peppers, seeded and cut into ½-inch strips
2 green bell peppers, seeded and cut into ½-inch strips
1 small head cauliflower, broken into small florets
18 small pearl onions, peeled, or 2 medium onions, peeled and quartered
½ can (6 oz. can) pitted black olives
½ cup pimiento-stuffed green olives
5-6 cloves garlic
5-6 small hot dried red chile peppers
6 cups water
1½ cups white vinegar
2 tbs. salt
2 tbs. mustard seeds
1 tsp. celery seeds
⅔ cup sugar

Sterilize 5 to 6 canning jars by submerging them in boiling water for 15 minutes; remove jars and air-dry. Submerge lids in boiling water for 3 minutes; remove and air-dry.

Layer a mixture of vegetables and olives in sterilized jars in an attractive arrangement, packing tightly. Place 1 clove garlic and 1 chile in each jar. Place remaining ingredients in a large pot, bring to a boil and boil for 3 minutes. Pour brine mixture into each jar until vegetables are covered. Clean jar tops well and seal with sterilized lids. Refrigerate for at least 2 weeks before serving.

MARINATED ASPARAGUS

If desired, this brine can be used for cauliflower or broccoli.

3 lb. fresh asparagus, tough ends removed
¾ cup cider vinegar or balsamic vinegar
1 tbs. dried dill weed
1 tbs. sugar
1 tbs. salt
1 tsp. pepper
2 cloves garlic, minced
1½ cups chicken stock or vegetable stock

Cut asparagus into bite-sized pieces and place in a shallow pan. Mix remaining ingredients together and pour over asparagus. Cover and refrigerate for 24 hours, turning occasionally. Drain before serving. Provide toothpicks for serving.

DILLED BROCCOLI AND CARROTS

This simple, colorful appetizer can also be used as a vegetable side dish. To make it even leaner, use 2 tbs. chicken stock instead of the butter and vegetable oil.

1 tbs. butter
1 tbs. vegetable oil
3-4 medium carrots, peeled and sliced
2 tbs. dry white wine
½ medium onion, sliced
1 cup fresh broccoli florets
½ tsp. dried dill weed
pepper to taste

In a large skillet, heat butter and oil over medium heat and sauté carrots for 1 minute. Add wine, cover and cook for 5 minutes. Add remaining ingredients, cover and simmer for 5 minutes, or until vegetables are tender-crisp. Serve warm. Provide toothpicks for serving.

MARINATED BLUE ONIONS

Makes 2½ cups

This recipe is fast to make, but you need to start a couple of days before you plan to serve it. Serve these with small rounds of rye or pumpernickel bread. Flat-shaped onions have a tendency to be sweeter than round ones.

½ cup extra virgin olive oil
2 tbs. lemon juice
1 tsp. salt
1 tsp. sugar
¼ cup crumbled blue cheese
dash pepper
dash paprika
2 cups finely sliced red onions
whole parsley sprigs or chopped fresh parsley for garnish

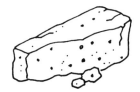

With a food processor or blender, process oil, lemon juice, salt, sugar, cheese, pepper and paprika until well blended. Place onions in a serving dish and cover with processed mixture. Cover dish with plastic wrap and chill for 2 days before serving. Garnish with parsley sprigs or a sprinkling of chopped parsley.

GRECIAN ARTICHOKES

Serve these savory morsels with crackers or bread rounds. This dish can also be used as a vegetable side dish by leaving the artichoke hearts whole.

¾ cup dry white wine
¾ cup water
¼ cup lemon juice
¼ cup extra virgin olive oil
2 bay leaves

¼ tsp. dried thyme
salt and pepper to taste
2 cans (14 oz. each) whole artichoke
    hearts, drained and quartered
1½ tbs. anchovy paste

In a saucepan, mix wine, water, lemon juice, olive oil, bay leaves, thyme, salt and pepper. Bring to a boil, reduce heat to low and simmer for about 6 minutes. Remove pan from heat, transfer ingredients to a bowl and cool to room temperature. Cover bowl and place in the refrigerator overnight.

Remove artichokes from marinade and set aside. Pour marinade into a saucepan, stir in anchovy paste and bring to a boil. Reduce heat to medium and cook until mixture thickens. Spoon thickened mixture over artichokes. Cool to room temperature and serve as is or chilled.

SPICED MELON BALLS

This cool, refreshing appetizer takes minutes to prepare and won't fill up your guests before dinner.

1 medium honeydew or Crenshaw melon
1 large cantaloupe
2 tbs. lime juice
2 tbs. honey
½ tsp. ground coriander
½ tsp. nutmeg
fresh mint sprigs or lime slices for garnish

Cut melons in half and remove seeds. With a melon baller, form fruit into balls and place in a bowl with remaining ingredients, stirring to coat melon balls. Cover bowl and chill for several hours before serving. Garnish with mint sprigs or lime slices. Provide toothpicks for serving.

MARINATED GOAT CHEESE

Serve these flavorful cheese cubes with toothpicks alongside Greek olives for nibbling. This recipe can also be served sliced as a first course with crusty French bread, as an accompaniment to a salad or as a stuffing for chicken breasts. It is pretty garnished with something red, such as finely chopped red bell pepper, crushed red pepper flakes, chopped fresh tomato or minced pimiento.

¼ cup chopped fresh parsley
1 tsp. dried basil
1 tsp. dried thyme
1 tsp. minced garlic

½ tsp. pepper
1 tbs. finely chopped fresh chives
1½ cups extra virgin olive oil
1 lb. French goat cheese, cut into cubes

In a bowl, mix together parsley, basil, thyme, garlic, pepper and chives. Heat oil in a small saucepan until just under the boiling point and pour hot oil over herbs. Let mixture come to room temperature and pour mixture over goat cheese in a shallow bowl. Cover bowl tightly and refrigerate for up to 3 days. Bring mixture to room temperature and pour off excess marinade before serving.

NOTE: Oil will turn cloudy and slightly solid when refrigerated. When brought to room temperature, it will turn clear and fluid once again.

CARAMELIZED NUTS

The secret to these nuts is soaking them in boiling water and drying them in the oven before beginning the caramelization process.

1 lb. whole shelled walnuts or pecans
boiling water
2 tbs. vegetable oil
1 tsp. coarse salt, or more if desired
¼-½ cup sugar

Place nuts in a heatproof bowl and cover with boiling water. Let stand for 30 minutes. Heat oven to 300°. Drain and rinse nuts well. Pat nuts dry with a towel and place on a baking sheet. Bake nuts for 30 minutes and stir. Reduce oven heat to 250° and bake nuts, checking and stirring every 10 minutes, until nuts no longer have moisture in the center. Remove from oven.

In a large skillet or wok, heat oil over medium heat. Add nuts to skillet, tossing to coat nuts; add salt and toss well. Add sugar, a little at a time, and stir until sugar begins to caramelize, about 3 to 4 minutes. Taste, taking care not to burn your mouth. Add more salt or sugar if needed. Remove caramelized nuts from heat and spread on buttered waxed paper to cool.

CURRIED CASHEWS

Cashews have a natural sweetness that goes well with curry flavors. Almonds can be substituted for the cashews if desired.

3 cups roasted salted or
   unsalted cashew nuts
¼ cup *Clarified Butter*, page 139
1 tsp. salt, optional
1½ tsp. curry powder
1 tsp. cumin powder

In a skillet over medium-high heat, sauté nuts in *Clarified Butter* until slightly browned. Add salt, if using unsalted nuts, curry powder and cumin and sauté, stirring constantly, until nuts are well browned. Transfer nuts to paper towels to drain. Cool slightly before serving.

TERIYAKI MIXED NUTS

The gentle flavor of these nuts can be enlivened by using 1 tsp. chopped fresh ginger in place of the powdered ginger. Use any type of nuts that suit your preference.

3 cups mixed whole shelled nuts
3 tbs. butter
1 tbs. soy sauce
2 tsp. lemon juice
1½ tsp. sugar
1 clove garlic, crushed
1 tsp. powdered ginger
salt to taste

Heat oven to 350°. Place nuts on a baking sheet in a single layer and bake until golden, about 8 to 10 minutes. Melt butter in medium saucepan. Stir in soy sauce, lemon juice, sugar, garlic, ginger and salt. Add toasted nuts to saucepan and stir to coat with butter mixture. Return coated nuts to baking sheet and bake for 6 to 8 minutes, stirring occasionally, until nuts are browned. Remove nuts from oven and cool slightly before serving.

CRISP PITA CHIPS

These unique chips can be flavored with an endless number of spices; use your imagination. Serve them with a dip or eat them like a flavored cracker.

10 pita breads
½ cup butter, melted
salt, optional
seasonings: dried herbs, spice powders or flavored salt blends, optional
topplngs: sesame seeds, grated Parmesan or Romano cheese, poppy seeds,
    bacon bits or caraway seeds, optional

Heat oven to 400°. For crisp chips, split pita breads horizontally, cut each round in half and each half into 3 wedges to yield 12 chips per pita bread. For chewy chips, do not separate pitas: Cut pita breads in half crosswise and cut each half into 3 wedges to yield 6 chips per pita bread.

Brush pita wedges with melted butter on both sides and sprinkle with salt, if using. Sprinkle one side of wedges with seasonings and/or toppings, if using (if making crisp pita chips, sprinkle items on the rougher side). Place chips on a baking sheet and bake for 10 to 12 minutes, until slightly brown. Chips will become more crisp as they cool.

CHEESE STRAWS

The addition of ginger makes these treats special. They make great nibblers at a wine party. For a fancy presentation, hold straws on both ends and twist in opposite directions before baking.

2 cups all-purpose flour
1 tsp. ground ginger
1 tsp. salt
2/3 cup cold butter, cut into small cubes
2 cups shredded sharp cheddar cheese
1/2 cup sesame seeds, toasted
1 tsp. Worcestershire sauce
4-5 tbs. cold water

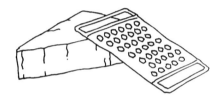

Heat oven to 400°. With a food processor or mixer, mix flour with ginger and salt. Add butter and cheese and process until blended. Add remaining ingredients, using enough water to form a stiff dough, and blend until dough forms a ball. Roll dough out on a floured surface until 1/8-inch thick and cut into 1/2-x-4-inch strips or "straws." Place straws on an ungreased baking sheet and bake for 10 to 12 minutes or until golden brown.

SWEET AND HOT DATE-WALNUT WAFERS

These popular treats can be frozen and brought out at a moment's notice.

8 oz. sharp cheddar cheese, shredded
1½ cups all-purpose flour
½ cup butter, softened
¼ tsp. cayenne pepper, or to taste
½ tsp. salt
¼ cup dry white wine
6 oz. pitted dates, chopped
1 cup walnuts, chopped
1 egg, beaten
toppings: ground walnuts, sesame seeds or grated Parmesan cheese, optional

With a food processor or pastry blender, mix cheese, flour, butter, cayenne and salt until mixture resembles cornmeal. Add wine and mix until moistened. Stir in dates and walnuts and form mixture into two 2-inch diameter logs. Roll each log in waxed paper and chill until ready to bake.

Heat oven to 375°. Cut logs into thin slices and brush slices with beaten egg. Sprinkle with toppings, if using. Bake for 10 to 12 minutes or until golden brown.

HOT AND COLD DIPS

ROASTED RED PEPPER DIP

Makes 2½ cups

Serve this dip with a beautiful array of fresh vegetables and garnish with fresh edible flowers and herbs. Look for whipped cream cheese in tubs in the super-market's dairy case.

2 green onions, chopped
1 jar (15 oz.) roasted red peppers, drained
1-2 tbs. lemon juice
1 cup whipped cream cheese

With a food processor or blender, process green onions until finely chopped. Add remaining ingredients and process until peppers are coarsely pureed and ingredients are well mixed. Chill until ready to use.

LOW-FAT CUCUMBER DIP

This refreshing dip goes well with vegetables or crackers.

1 medium cucumber, peeled,
   halved lengthwise and seeded
salt
⅓ cup low-fat or nonfat cottage cheese
1 cup plain low-fat or nonfat yogurt
1 tbs. chopped fresh parsley
½ tsp. dried dill weed, or more to taste
¼ tsp. white pepper, or more to taste

With a food processor or box grater, shred cucumber. Place cucumber shreds in a colander, sprinkle with salt and let stand over the sink for 30 minutes. Remove cucumber from colander and squeeze dry with paper towels. Process remaining ingredients with a food processor or blender until smooth. Stir in cucumber, taste and adjust seasonings. Cover and refrigerate until ready to serve.

TOMATO SALSA

This is a must to serve with tortilla chips — freshly made if you've got the time. It's also good with bean dishes, vegetable salads and chicken. For a low-fat dipper, cut corn tortillas into wedges and bake in a 350° oven for 10 minutes or until crisp.

1 medium sweet onion, such as Bermuda, chopped
3 cloves garlic, minced
½ green bell pepper, chopped
½ red bell pepper, chopped
½ cup chopped fresh cilantro
2 tbs. lemon juice
2 tsp. sugar
2 cups fresh seeded and chopped tomatoes, or
    1 can (15 oz.) Mexican-style stewed tomatoes
salt and pepper to taste
chopped fresh jalapeño pepper to taste, optional

Place all ingredients in a food processor workbowl or blender container and process with a pulsing action until just blended. Do not puree mixture; texture should be chunky. Taste and adjust seasonings.

GUACAMOLE

Save the avocado pit and imbed it in the center of this mixture until you're ready to serve — this will help to keep the avocados from discoloring. Serve this dip with tortilla chips, corn chips, vegetables or tortillas wedges.

4 large, ripe Hass avocados, peeled and pitted
juice of 2 limes
½ cup shredded cheddar cheese
½ cup chopped Bermuda onion
dash salt
1 jalapeño pepper, seeded and
   chopped, optional
1 tbs. chopped fresh cilantro
1-2 tomatoes, seeded and chopped
chopped fresh cilantro for garnish

With a food processor or blender, process 3 of the avocados until smooth. Add lime juice, cheese, onion, salt, jalapeño and 1 tbs. cilantro and pulse briefly to blend. Taste and adjust seasonings. With a knife, cut remaining avocado into small chunks. Add avocado chunks to pureed mixture with chopped tomatoes stir until incorporated. Place in a serving bowl and sprinkle with cilantro.

CREAMY AVOCADO VEGGIE DIP

Makes 2½ cups

Offer a gorgeous array of colorful vegetables to serve beside this delicious dip. It also goes well with tortilla chips or crisp bagel chips.

1½ tsp. balsamic or red wine vinegar
1½ tbs. lemon juice
½ cup olive oil
1 tbs. Dijon mustard
¼ cup minced green onions
1 tsp. salt
½ tsp. sugar

freshly ground pepper to taste
8 oz. cream cheese, softened
2 cloves garlic, minced
1 large ripe Hass avocado, peeled and
  pitted
2 tbs. chopped fresh parsley

With a food processor or blender, process vinegar, lemon juice, olive oil, mustard, 2 tbs. of the green onions, salt, sugar and pepper until smooth; remove mixture and set aside. Add cream cheese, garlic and avocado to machine and process until smooth and creamy. With machine running, very slowly pour vinegar mixture in a thin stream into cream cheese mixture and process until smooth. Transfer to a serving bowl and stir in remaining 2 tbs. green onions and parsley.

SWEET POTATO AND CARROT DIP

Makes 4 cups

Dip into this piquant, yet sweet, vegetable dip with freshly cut vegetables or pita bread. You can steam the vegetables rather than boiling them to retain more of their nutrients.

1 lb. sweet potatoes or yams, peeled and cut into chunks
1 lb. carrots, peeled and cut into chunks
1 tsp. salt
3 cloves garlic
1 tsp. ground cumin
1 tsp. cinnamon
3-4 tbs. olive oil or vegetable stock
3 tbs. balsamic or red wine vinegar
pinch cayenne pepper, or more to taste
salt to taste

Place sweet potatoes and carrots in a saucepan with 1 tsp. salt and cover with water. Bring to a boil, reduce heat to low and simmer until vegetables are soft, about 15 minutes; drain. Puree cooked vegetables with a food processor or blender. Add remaining ingredients and process until blended. Taste and adjust seasonings.

GARBANZO BEAN DIP (HUMMUS)

This dip is quick to put together and is ideally served with fresh or toasted pita bread wedges. Tahini can be found in health food stores, Middle Eastern markets and some supermarkets.

1 tbs. olive oil
1 small onion, chopped
2-3 cloves garlic, minced
2 cups drained canned garbanzo beans
½ tsp. turmeric
2 tbs. chopped fresh parsley
1-2 tbs. lemon juice, or to taste
2-3 tbs. tahini (sesame seed paste), optional
water, optional

In a skillet, heat olive oil over medium heat and sauté onion and garlic until soft and transparent. Rinse garbanzo beans with cold water and drain well. Place all ingredients in a blender container or food processor workbowl and puree to the consistency of mayonnaise. If mixture is too thick, add a small amount of water.

SMOKY EGGPLANT DIP (BABA GHANOUSH)

This very healthy and tasty eggplant dip originated in the Middle East. The trick to this dish is in the smoky flavor obtained from scraping the charred eggplant skins. If you prefer a little heat, add a dash of cayenne pepper. Accompany this dip with pita bread wedges or strips of Middle Eastern flatbread.

2 large eggplants, halved lengthwise
salt to taste
2 cloves garlic, finely minced
¼ cup chopped onion
lime or lemon juice to taste
1½ tbs. tahini (sesame seed paste)
2 tbs. chopped fresh parsley

Heat broiler. Place eggplants cut-side down on a baking sheet. Broil eggplants for 15 to 20 minutes, until skin is blackened and flesh is softened. Remove eggplant from oven, sprinkle cut side of eggplant with salt and place eggplant in a colander to drain for about 15 minutes. Scrape flesh from eggplant skin, scraping some charred bits of skin into mixture for flavor. Puree eggplant pulp and remaining ingredients with a food processor or blender until smooth. Taste and adjust seasonings. Refrigerate until ready to serve.

GREEK FISH ROE DIP (TARAMASALATA)

Serve this creamy dip with toasted bread or pita bread. Tarama can be found in Greek delis or specialty food stores.

⅓ jar (8 oz. jar) tarama (fish roe)
1 small onion, finely grated
about 1½ cups olive oil, or more if desired
5 slices white bread, crusts removed, moistened with a small amount of water
⅓ cup fresh lemon juice, or to taste
chopped fresh oregano for garnish

Place tarama and onion in a bowl and mash with a fork. Add a small amount of olive oil very slowly to create a paste. Squeeze excess water from bread. with a whisk, beat bread into tarama mixture alternately with remaining olive oil and lemon juice until a creamy mixture is obtained. Stop adding olive oil when desired thickness is reached. Taste and adjust seasonings. Serve garnished with fresh oregano.

CLAM DIP

Because of the uncomplicated recipe, the clam flavor in this quick dip can be fully appreciated. Serve it with chips, crackers or bread rounds.

1 can (6 oz.) minced clams
8 oz. cream cheese, softened
1 tbs. Worcestershire sauce
1 tsp. lemon juice, or more to taste

Drain clams and reserve juice. Mix clams with remaining ingredients. Taste and add more lemon if desired. For a thinner dip, add a small amount of clam juice until desired consistency is reached.

HOT CLAM DIP

The flavor of this unusual combination will really surprise you. Serve it with crackers or bread rounds.

⅔ cup finely chopped onion
2 tbs. butter
½ cup chopped green bell pepper
½ lb. processed American cheese, cut into cubes
¼ cup ketchup
1 tbs. Worcestershire sauce
1½ tsp. dry sherry
dash Tabasco sauce or cayenne pepper
2 cans (6.5 oz. each) chopped clams, drained

In a small saucepan over medium heat, sauté onion and pepper in butter until slightly wilted. Add remaining ingredients, except clams, and stir until cheese is melted. Stir in clams, taste and adjust seasonings. Transfer to a heatproof bowl set over a candle warmer, or to a fondue pot. Serve immediately. Keep warm.

HOT GARLIC AND ANCHOVY DIP (BAGNA CAUDA)

This creamy variation of a traditional Italian dip goes well with freshly cut vegetables or bread rounds for dipping.

¼ cup butter
6-8 anchovy fillets, finely chopped
4 cloves garlic, minced
2 cups heavy cream
1 tbs. cornstarch
2 tbs. water

Melt butter in a saucepan over medium heat. Add chopped anchovies and garlic and sauté for a few minutes. Add cream to pan and heat until just below the boiling point. In a small bowl, mix cornstarch with water and add to saucepan, stirring until thickened. Transfer to a heatproof bowl set over a candle warmer, or to a fondue pot. Serve immediately. Keep warm.

WARM SWEET PEPPER DIP

This quick, colorful, hot dip goes well with crackers, pita crisps or bagel chips.

8 oz. cream cheese, softened
½ cup shredded Parmesan cheese
1 small onion, diced
1 tbs. chopped fresh basil
1 red bell pepper, seeded and cut into chunks
1 green bell pepper, seeded and cut into chunks
1 yellow bell pepper, seeded and cut into chunks

Heat oven to 350°. With a food processor or blender, process cream cheese with Parmesan until fluffy. Add onion and basil and process until mixed. Add peppers to cream cheese mixture and process until well mixed. Transfer to a shallow baking dish and bake for 15 minutes. Serve warm in a chafing dish or on a hot plate.

HOT BEAN AND BACON DIP

This simple dip takes just minutes to prepare and goes well with an assortment of vegetables, chips or even bread cubes. If you like it on the spicy side, increase the amount of chili powder and Tabasco sauce to taste.

1 can (11½ oz.) bean
    and bacon soup
6 oz. processed American
    cheese, cut into cubes
¼ cup finely chopped
    onion or green onions
⅛ tsp. Tabasco sauce,
    or more to taste
chili powder for garnish

In a saucepan over medium heat, stir together soup, cheese and onions until cheese melts. Stir in Tabasco sauce and sprinkle with chili powder. Transfer to a heatproof bowl set over a candle warmer, or to a fondue pot. Serve immediately. Keep warm.

HOT CHEESE AND BACON DIP

This fast, delicious dip goes well with crusty French bread, breadsticks or crackers as accompaniments.

½ lb. bacon, cut into small pieces
1 can (8 oz.) tomato sauce
¼ cup finely chopped onion
½ tsp. minced garlic
⅛ tsp. pepper
¾ cup shredded cheddar cheese, or 6 oz. processed
   American cheese, cut into small cubes

Cook bacon in a small skillet over medium-high heat until crisp and transfer to paper towels to drain. Drain off most of the bacon fat from skillet and add tomato sauce, onion, garlic and pepper and simmer for 5 minutes. Add cheese and stir until melted. Crumble bacon and stir into skillet. Transfer to a heatproof bowl set over a candle warmer, or to a fondue pot. Serve immediately. Keep warm.

SMOKY CHEESE FONDUE

Make this recipe with smoked cheddar cheese, smoked Swiss cheese or a combination of both — all variations are great. Serve with toasted bread cubes or wedges of pears and apples for dunking. For an additional treat, offer pieces of cooked bacon.

2 tbs. butter
2 tbs. flour
1 tsp. Dijon mustard, or more to taste
2 cups warm milk, or more if needed
¾ lb. smoked cheddar and/or smoked Swiss cheese, shredded
½ cup sweet white wine

In a fondue pot or nonaluminum saucepan, melt butter over medium-high heat. Stir in flour and mustard until bubbling. Add milk and whisk until thickened. Add cheese and stir until melted. Just before serving, stir in wine. Keep mixture warm in fondue pot, or transfer to a heatproof bowl and keep warm with an electric warming tray or candle warmer. If mixture begins to thicken, stir in a little more warm milk.

CRAB FONDUE

This delicious, creamy dip is best served with French bread rounds or plain crackers. Use enough paprika to achieve the color and flavor that you desire. Serve it warm in a chafing dish.

2 tbs. butter
½ cup chopped white or
    brown mushrooms
¼ cup cream sherry
salt and pepper to taste
dash cayenne pepper
paprika to taste
3 egg yolks, beaten
1 cup heavy cream
1 lb. crabmeat

Melt butter in a skillet over medium-high heat and sauté mushrooms until tender. Carefully add sherry, salt, pepper, cayenne and paprika to skillet and stir to combine. Add egg yolks and cream to skillet and stir over medium heat until mixture thickens. Stir in crabmeat. Transfer to a heatproof bowl set over a candle warmer, or to a fondue pot. Serve immediately. Keep warm.

CHOCOLATE AMARETTO FONDUE

Serve this in a fondue pot surrounded by chunks of fresh fruit, such as bananas, pineapple, apples, pears and strawberries, as well as pieces of angel food and pound cake. To really impress your guests, offer a variety of chopped toasted nuts, such as almonds, pecans, walnuts or cashews for dipping into after coating the morsels with chocolate.

12 oz. milk chocolate, chopped, or milk chocolate chips
¾ cup heavy cream
3 tbs. amaretto liqueur, or to taste, or 1 tsp. almond extract
fresh fruit, cut into 1-inch chunks, for dipping
angel food cake or pound cake, cut into 1-inch chunks, for dipping

Place chocolate and cream in the top of a double boiler over hot, not boiling, water and stir until chocolate melts mixture is blended. Stir in amaretto. Transfer to a heatproof bowl set over a candle warmer, or to a fondue pot. Serve immediately. Keep warm. Serve with chopped fruit and/or cake.

SPREADS, MOUSSES AND PATÉS

APRICOT SPREAD

Makes 4 cups

Serve this sweet spread with tea breads. Or, mix it with cream cheese to serve as a spread for mini-bagels.

1 lb. dried apricots
apricot or apple juice to cover
pinch ground anise
2 tbs. arrowroot or cornstarch
2 cups apple juice
pinch salt

Place apricots in a heavy saucepan with apricot juice and anise. Simmer over low heat until apricots are soft, about 30 minutes. Transfer mixture to a food processor workbowl or blender container and puree until smooth; return mixture to saucepan and bring back to a simmer. Mix arrowroot or cornstarch with apple juice and stir into apricot mixture until thickened. Add salt, taste and adjust seasonings. Cool mixture and refrigerate until ready to use.

OLIVE SPREAD (TAPENADE)

This is a perfect dish to take to a party. Serve with thin baguette rounds or freshly made breadsticks.

2 cans (6 oz. each) pitted black olives
3 tbs. capers
½ cup minced onion
1 tsp. minced garlic
2 tbs. chopped fresh parsley
¼ cup grated Parmesan cheese
2 tbs. olive oil
2 tbs. balsamic or red wine vinegar
½ tsp. salt, or more to taste
½ tsp. pepper, or more to taste
¼ cup chopped red bell pepper

With a food processor or blender, barely chop olives; transfer olives to a bowl. Place remaining ingredients, except 2 tbs. of the bell pepper, in workbowl and process until minced. Transfer mixture to bowl with olives and stir until well mixed. Taste and adjust seasonings. Garnish with remaining red pepper.

OLIVE CROSTINI SPREAD

Makes 1½ cups

This piquant Italian favorite can be quite filling. Serve it on toasted bread rounds. If desired, sprinkle with a little grated Parmesan cheese and broil until the cheese is melted.

1 can (6 oz.) pitted black olives
1 tbs. minced onion
2 tbs. minced fresh parsley
2 tbs. lemon juice
2 cloves garlic, minced
4 anchovies
¼ cup olive oil
salt and pepper to taste

Process all ingredients with a blender or food processor until barely mixed. Taste and adjust seasonings. Chill until ready to serve.

AVOCADO OLIVE SPREAD

Serve this spread cold with raw vegetables. Or, spread it on toasted bread rounds, top with shredded Swiss cheese and broil until the cheese is melted.

12 oz. cream cheese, softened
1 ripe Hass avocado
1 tsp. lemon juice
1 cup finely chopped black olives
1 tbs. chopped fresh parsley
1/3 cup chopped tomatoes
1/4 cup finely chopped celery

With a food processor or mixer, blend cream cheese until smooth. Peel avocado, remove pit and mash in a bowl with lemon juice. Add avocado mixture to food processor and puree until smooth. Add remaining ingredients and mix until just combined. Chill until ready to use.

SWEET PEPPER ANTIPASTO (PEPERONATA)

This healthy Italian appetizer has wonderful eye-appeal. Serve it with toasted bread rounds.

2-3 green bell peppers, halved and seeded
2 yellow bell peppers, halved and seeded
2 red bell peppers, halved and seeded
3 fresh tomatoes, diced
1 tsp. salt
1 tbs. minced fresh parsley
½ cup black olives
2 tbs. capers or chopped anchovies, optional
2 cloves garlic, mashed

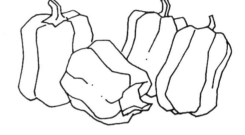

Heat broiler. Place peppers cut-side down on a baking sheet and broil until skins turn black. Let peppers stand until cool enough to handle and peel off charred skin. Dice peppers and place in a bowl with tomatoes, salt, parsley, olives, capers and garlic; mix well. Chill until ready to serve, stirring occasionally. Discard garlic before serving.

EGGPLANT ANTIPASTO (CAPONATA)

Serve this fresh vegetable spread hot or cold with rounds of crusty French bread. It can also be used as a vegetable side dish.

1 medium eggplant, peeled and diced
salt
¼ cup olive oil
1 medium zucchini, diced
1 large onion, diced
3 cloves garlic, minced
½ cup diced celery
1 large carrot, diced
1 green bell pepper, seeded and diced
1½ cups chopped tomatoes, drained

3 tbs. tomato paste
¼ cup chopped fresh parsley
½ tsp. dried basil
¼ cup red wine vinegar
2 tsp. sugar
¼ cup chopped stuffed green olives
¼ cup chopped pitted black olives
2 tbs. coarsely chopped capers
salt and pepper to taste

Place eggplant in a colander and sprinkle lightly with salt; let stand for about 30 minutes until some of the moisture has drained off. Heat oil in large skillet over medium-high heat and sauté eggplant zucchini and until lightly browned. Stir in onion, garlic, celery and carrot and sauté for about 10 minutes. Add remaining ingredients, reduce heat to low and simmer gently for about 1 hour. Taste and adjust seasonings. Serve hot or cold.

EGGPLANT CAVIAR

Serve this healthy mixture with an assortment of crackers or sliced bread.

2 eggplants
1 tbs. olive oil
2 cloves garlic
1 small onion, quartered
1 red bell pepper, seeded and quartered
1 green bell pepper, seeded and quartered
1 tomato, peeled and seeded
1 tbs. capers

1 tbs. fresh lemon juice
1/8 tsp. Tabasco Sauce
1 tsp. salt
1/4 tsp. pepper
3 tbs. balsamic or red wine vinegar
1 tsp. dried basil
1/4 cup olive oil or vegetable stock
1/2 cup chopped black olives
1/2 cup chopped green olives

Heat oven to 350°. Brush eggplants with olive oil and bake until soft, about 30 minutes; cool, cut in half and scoop out flesh. Reserve 1 eggplant shell if desired. Mince garlic with a food processor or blender. Add onion and peppers and pulse to coarsely chop; remove and set aside. Add tomato, eggplant pulp, capers, lemon juice, Tabasco, salt, pepper, vinegar, basil and 1/4 cup oil to machine and process until well mixed. Add coarsely chopped vegetables and process just until mixed. Transfer mixture to a heavy saucepan and cook over medium heat for 20 minutes. Stir in olives and adjust seasonings. Chill. If desired, serve in eggplant shell.

MANGO CHUTNEY MOLD

Cover crackers or plain bagel chips with this creamy, sweet, exotic spread.

12 oz. cream cheese, softened
3 tbs. mayonnaise
3 tbs. chopped peanuts
3-4 tbs. chopped raisins
4 slices bacon, cooked until crisp
  and crumbled
1 tbs. chopped green onions
2 tsp. curry powder
1 cup mango chutney
½ cup shredded coconut

With a food processor or mixer, process cream cheese with mayonnaise until smooth. Add peanuts, raisins, bacon, green onions and curry powder and pulse until blended. Lightly oil a 3-cup mold and fill with cream cheese mixture. Chill for several hours or overnight.

Briefly chop chutney with a food processor or knife to make sure there are no large pieces of fruit. To serve, invert cream cheese mixture onto a serving plate, pour chutney on top and sprinkle with coconut.

CHUTNEY AND CHEESE SPREAD

Chutney and curry powder create a spicy, savory taste sensation. Serve this spread with crisp crackers.

8 oz. cream cheese, softened
4 oz. cheddar cheese, shredded
2 tbs. brandy
1 tsp. curry powder, or to taste
1 jar (8 oz.) mango chutney
½ cup chopped toasted almonds for garnish
2 green onions, chopped, for garnish

With a food processor or mixer, process cream cheese, cheddar cheese, brandy and curry powder until mixture is light and fluffy. Taste and adjust seasonings. Transfer mixture to a serving dish and cover with chutney. Chill until ready to serve. Garnish with chopped almonds and green onions.

MOLDED HERBED CHEESE SPREAD

Shape this spread into molds to fit the theme of your party. Or, consider using it to stuff celery sticks or spread on small, shaped bread slices.

16 oz. cream cheese, softened
6 green onions, chopped
4 cloves garlic, minced
½ cup chopped fresh parsley
½ cup chopped fresh basil
1 tsp. dry mustard
1 tsp. Worcestershire sauce
¼ cup lemon juice
½ cup chopped black olives
salt and pepper to taste

With a food processor or mixer, process ingredients together until blended. Taste and adjust seasonings. Spoon mixture into an oiled 3-cup mold, cover and refrigerate until mixture is firm. To serve, invert mixture onto a serving platter.

GORGONZOLA SPREAD

This is a great spread to serve with toasted bread slices or thin pear slices. Gorgonzola is a pungent variety of blue cheese.

8 oz. cream cheese, softened
2 oz. Gorgonzola cheese, crumbled
2 tbs. butter, softened
2 tbs. chopped green onions
2 tbs. dry sherry
½ lb. bacon, cooked until crisp and crumbled,
   or ½ cup chopped toasted walnuts

In a bowl, mix cream cheese, Gorgonzola cheese, butter, green onions and sherry until well blended. Stir in bacon and chill until ready to serve.

ROQUEFORT MOUSSE

This tantalizing spread is delicious served with an assortment of crackers and fruit. It goes especially well with sliced pears.

1 cup cold heavy cream
2 eggs, separated
1 lb. Roquefort cheese, room
   temperature
8 oz. cream cheese, softened

½ cup butter, softened
2 tbs. unflavored gelatin
¼ cup cold water
1 tsp. Dijon mustard

In a chilled bowl, whip cream until stiff and set aside. In another bowl, beat egg whites until stiff and set aside. In a large bowl, beat egg yolks until pale yellow, add Roquefort and beat until smooth. Add cream cheese and butter and beat until smooth. In a small saucepan, dissolve gelatin in cold water; gently heat mixture and stir until gelatin is completely dissolved. Add gelatin mixture to cream cheese mixture with mustard and stir until blended. Fold in beaten egg whites. Fold in whipped cream. Pour mixture into an oiled 7-cup mold and chill until firm. At serving time, invert mixture onto a serving platter.

NOTE: If you are concerned about the raw eggs in your area, increase cream to 1½ cups and substitute ¼ cup pasteurized eggs, such as Egg Beaters, for egg yolks.

SPREADS, MOUSSES AND PATÉS   55

BLUE CHEESECAKE

Serve this unique appetizer with rye bread rounds or crackers. Garnish with colorful edible flowers or carved vegetable flowers. Or, consider garnishing with a sprinkling of minced red bell pepper and green onions.

16 oz. cream cheese, softened
8 oz. blue cheese, crumbled
¼ tsp. white pepper
2½ cups sour cream

3 eggs
½ cup chopped toasted pecans
¼ cup minced green onions

Heat oven to 300°. With a food processor or blender, process cream cheese, blue cheese and white pepper until well blended. Add 1 cup of the sour cream and eggs and process until just mixed. Stir in pecans and green onions. Pour mixture into a buttered 9-inch springform pan and bake for 65 minutes. Remove from oven and let stand for 5 minutes. Spread remaining 1½ cups sour cream over the top of cheesecake and return to oven for 10 minutes. Cool completely and refrigerate overnight.

To serve, remove sides of springform and place cheesecake on a serving platter.

GOAT CHEESE, PESTO AND SUN-DRIED TOMATO TERRINE

This recipe looks complicated, but it can be thrown together in minutes. It has beautiful eye-appeal. Serve with crackers or sliced baguettes.

2 lb. cream cheese, softened
8 oz. goat cheese, crumbled
1 jar (8.5 oz.) oil-packed
    sun-dried tomatoes, drained
1 jar (10 oz.) basil pesto

In a bowl, mix cream cheese with goat cheese until well blended. Line a terrine mold or loaf pan with a piece of wet cheesecloth. Spread ⅕ of the cheese mixture evenly in pan and cover with ½ of the tomatoes. Spread another ⅕ of the cheese mixture over tomatoes and cover with ½ of the pesto. Repeat layers, ending with cheese mixture. Chill for several hours or overnight.

To serve, invert mixture onto a serving platter and remove cheesecloth.

SWEET AND SAVORY STUFFED BRIE

Serve this easy-to-fix appetizer with apple wedges and mild crackers. If desired, garnish with unpeeled apple slices and walnut halves. To prevent the apple slices from turning brown, dip them in a mixture of lemon juice and water.

1 large wheel (about 6 lb.)
  Brie cheese
2 medium Golden Delicious apples,
  peeled, cored and chopped
1¼ cups brown sugar, packed
¼-½ cup crumbled blue cheese
1 cup chopped toasted walnuts

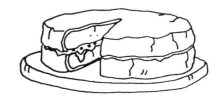

Heat oven to 325°. Slice Brie in half horizontally. In a bowl, combine apples, brown sugar, blue cheese and walnuts. Spread apple mixture on one cut-side of Brie and place remaining Brie half on top, cut-side down. Place filled Brie on an ovenproof platter and bake for about 20 minutes. Serve warm.

BRIE IN WINE ASPIC

Brie decorated in this fashion makes a really pretty, very impressive appetizer that will wow your friends. Serve with special crackers or rounds of French bread. Aspic is a savory jelly made from flavored liquid and gelatin. It is commonly used in French cuisine.

2 pkg. (¼ oz. each) unflavored gelatin
½ cup cold water
2 cups dry white wine
1 large wheel (about 6 lb.) Brie cheese
pansies or other edible flowers for garnish

For aspic, dissolve gelatin in cold water in a small saucepan; gently heat mixture and stir until gelatin is completely dissolved. Remove pan from heat and stir in wine. Let mixture cool slightly. Place Brie on a decorative serving platter. With a pastry brush, brush a layer of aspic on top and along sides of Brie. Artfully arrange flowers on top of Brie and gently brush with aspic. Chill for 5 minutes in the refrigerator. Brush another layer of aspic on top (not on sides) of Brie and chill for 5 minutes. Repeat brushing and chilling steps several times, until flowers are completely immersed in aspic. Chill until ready to serve.

VEGETABLE-STUFFED BRIE

This beautiful, elegant treatment for Brie can be made ahead of time. Serve with rounds of crisp French bread or crackers.

1 large wheel (about 6 lb.) Brie cheese
2 cloves garlic, minced
1 small onion, chopped
1 tbs. butter
8 large white or brown mushrooms, finely chopped
½ jar (4 oz. jar) roasted red bell peppers, chopped

1 can (4 oz.) sliced black olives
1 tbs. dry sherry
salt and pepper to taste
chopped fresh parsley for garnish, optional
chopped red and green bell pepper for garnish, optional

Slice Brie in half horizontally and chill until ready to use. In a skillet, sauté garlic and onion in butter until tender. Add mushrooms, peppers and olives and sauté for 3 minutes. Add sherry and season with salt and pepper.

One hour before serving, place one half of Brie cut-side up on a serving platter. Spread warm filling over cut-side of Brie and cover with remaining Brie half, cut-side down. If desired, garnish top of Brie with parsley or bell peppers.

CRUNCHY HAM AND CHEESE BALL

Serve this ham-infused cheese ball with an assortment of crackers. Waiting until the last minute to roll the cheese ball in nuts preserves the nuts' crunchy quality.

8 oz. cream cheese, softened
¼ cup mayonnaise
1 green onion, finely chopped
2 tbs. chopped fresh parsley
¼ tsp. dry mustard
¼ tsp. Tabasco Sauce
2 cups finely chopped cooked ham
1 cup chopped toasted walnuts

With a food processor or mixer, mix all ingredients, except nuts, until blended. Form mixture into a ball, wrap with plastic wrap and chill until ready to serve. Just before serving, remove plastic wrap and roll ball in nuts.

LATTICE CREAM CHEESE MOLD

This favorite spread is fancy enough to take to a party. For a change, use different complementary combinations of cheeses and meats. Serve with an assortment of crisp crackers.

FIRST LAYER

8 oz. cream cheese, softened
2 tbs. butter, softened
6 oz. smoked ham, minced
2 dashes Tabasco Sauce

SECOND LAYER

8 oz. cream cheese, softened
2 tbs. butter, softened
⅓ lb. sharp cheddar cheese, grated
2 tbs. milk or cream
few drops orange food coloring,
    optional

THIRD LAYER

8 oz. cream cheese, softened
2 tbs. butter, softened
4 green onions, tops only, finely minced
few drops green food coloring, optional

GARNISH

4 oz. cream cheese, softened
sliced black olives
sliced pimientos

Line a 9-inch springform pan with plastic wrap. With a food processor or blender, process first layer ingredients until blended. Spread mixture evenly in lined pan and place pan in the freezer.

With food processor, process second layer ingredients until blended. When first layer is firm, spread second layer on top and return pan to freezer.

With food processor, process third layer ingredients until blended. When second layer is firm, spread third layer on top. Cover pan with plastic and refrigerate until well set, at least 1 hour. When ready to serve, remove sides of springform and place mold on a serving platter; green layer should be on top.

For garnish, whip 4 oz. cream cheese until fluffy and place in a pastry bag with a small plain tip. Pipe thin stripes of cream cheese in a criss-cross pattern across the top of mold. Place black olives and pimiento slices at each intersecting line, alternating colors.

SIMPLE LIVER PATÉ

The traditional way to serve paté is to accompany it with cocktail onions, gherkin pickles and, of course, sliced crusty French bread.

1 lb. bacon
1½ cups chopped onions
1 lb. calves liver, cut into 1-inch cubes
1 lb. chicken livers, cut in half
2 tsp. salt, or to taste
1 tsp. pepper
3 egg yolks
2 eggs
¼ cup Madeira or red wine
¾ tsp. dried chervil
½ tsp. dried tarragon
½ tsp. nutmeg
¼ tsp. ground allspice

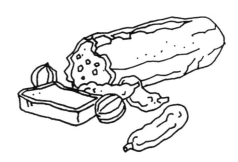

Line a loaf pan or a 7-inch soufflé mold with all but 6 of the bacon slices. Dice remaining 6 bacon slices and cook in a large skillet until browned. Add onions to skillet and sauté until onions are slightly browned. Add calves liver, chicken livers, 1 tsp. of the salt and ½ tsp. of the pepper and sauté until livers are no longer pink. Cool slightly.

Heat oven to 375°. With a food processor or blender, puree liver mixture, a little at a time, until smooth. Add egg yolks, eggs, Madeira, chervil, tarragon, nutmeg, allspice and remaining salt and pepper to machine and process until well mixed. Taste and adjust seasonings. Pour mixture into bacon-lined loaf pan and cover with foil. Place loaf pan in a larger baking pan and add water until it comes halfway up the sides of loaf pan. Bake paté in water bath for 2 hours. Carefully remove pans from oven, remove loaf pan and pour off any excess fat; cool. Cover paté with a new piece of foil and place a weight, such as a brick, on top. Refrigerate for at least 8 hours before serving.

To serve, remove weight and invert paté onto a serving platter.

PATÉ WITH ASPARAGUS

*This pork- and beef-based paté has asparagus dotted throughout. Serve it with crusty French bread and **Asparagus Mayonnaise** to dollop on top.*

1 lb. ground pork
1 lb. lean ground beef chuck
1 cup fresh breadcrumbs
1 pkg. (10 oz.) frozen chopped spinach, thawed and squeezed dry
1 tsp. dried sage
1 tsp. dried thyme
2 tsp. salt
1 tsp. pepper

1 tsp. ground rosemary
2 cloves garlic, minced
1 tbs. chopped fresh parsley
6 spears fresh asparagus, tough ends trimmed
lettuce leaves
Asparagus Mayonnaise, follows
chopped fresh parsley for garnish

Heat oven to 350°. In a bowl, thoroughly mix pork, beef, breadcrumbs, spinach, seasonings, garlic and parsley. Place meat mixture in a loaf pan, arranging asparagus spears in a random pattern throughout. Bake for 45 to 55 minutes, until a thermometer reads 170° when inserted into the center. Remove paté from oven and cool. Cover paté with aluminum foil and place a weight, such as a brick, on top. Refrigerate overnight.

To serve, remove weight and invert paté onto a plate. Cut paté into slices and place on a serving platter lined with lettuce. Spoon a strip of *Asparagus Mayonnaise* down the center of paté slices and sprinkle with chopped parsley. Place remaining *Asparagus Mayonnaise* in a small dish to serve as an accompaniment.

ASPARAGUS MAYONNAISE
Makes 2 cups

This can also be used as a dressing for pasta salads or as a spread for sandwiches. Or, it can mixed into a filling for deviled eggs.

¼ lb. asparagus
1½ cups purchased mayonnaise
¼ tsp. dry mustard
salt and pepper to taste

Steam asparagus until very tender, about 6 to 8 minutes; cool. With a blender or food processor, puree asparagus until smooth. Add mayonnaise and mustard and process briefly, just until blended. Taste and adjust seasonings. Chill until ready to use.

CREAMY CRAB SPREAD

Serve this stylish appetizer with plain crackers or bread rounds so that the delicate flavor of the crab can be fully appreciated.

3 hard-cooked egg yolks
½ cup butter, softened
½ cup mayonnaise
1 clove garlic, minced
1 tsp. Dijon mustard
dash prepared horseradish sauce

¼ cup minced green onions
¼ cup minced fresh parsley
12 oz. fresh crabmeat
2 tbs. fresh lemon juice
salt and white pepper to taste

With a food processor or blender, process egg yolks, butter, mayonnaise, garlic, mustard, horseradish, green onions and parsley until smooth. Transfer mixture to a bowl and gently stir in crabmeat, lemon juice, salt and white pepper. Taste and adjust seasonings. Place in a covered container and refrigerate until ready to serve.

MOLDED CRAB AND AVOCADO SPREAD

If you're feeling extravagant, garnish the center and edges of the mold with extra crabmeat. Serve with crisp crackers or toasted bread rounds.

2 pkg. (¼ oz. each) unflavored gelatin
1 cup cold water
4 ripe Hass avocados
1 cup mayonnaise
1 cup sour cream
2-3 tbs. finely minced onion

¼ cup fresh lemon juice
1 tsp. salt
dash cayenne pepper
½ tsp. Dijon mustard
18 oz. crabmeat
additional crabmeat for garnish, optional

In a small saucepan, dissolve gelatin in cold water. Gently heat mixture and stir until gelatin is completely dissolved; cool. In a bowl, mash avocados. Stir in cooled gelatin mixture, mayonnaise, sour cream, onion, lemon juice, salt, cayenne and mustard until well mixed. Gently fold in crabmeat and pour mixture into an oiled 4-cup mold. Cover and refrigerate for 8 hours. Invert mold onto a serving platter and garnish with additional crabmeat, if desired.

EASY CRABMEAT SPREAD

This quick, sophisticated dish goes well with crackers, crusty bread rounds or melba toast. If desired, garnish with a few whole crab legs.

8 oz. cream cheese, softened
2 green onions, finely chopped
2 tbs. lemon juice
¼ tsp. paprika
¼ tsp. white pepper
⅛ tsp. cayenne pepper
¼ tsp. salt
12 oz. crabmeat

With a food processor or blender, process all ingredients, except crabmeat, until smooth. Transfer mixture to a serving bowl and stir in crabmeat. Chill until ready to serve.

SARDINE AND PEPPER SPREAD

Serve this typical Spanish "tapa" with crusty bread rounds or crackers.

2 pkg. (3.75 oz. each) sardines packed in oil
½ cup extra virgin olive oil
2 medium onions, chopped
1 jar (4 oz.) roasted red bell peppers, drained and cut into strips
salt to taste

Heat oven to 350°. Rinse sardines with warm water and drain. Pour ¼ cup of the olive oil into a small baking dish and layer with onions, sardines and red peppers. Sprinkle with remaining olive oil and salt. Bake for 30 minutes, until hot throughout. Serve warm on bread or crackers.

QUICK SMOKED SALMON LOG

This creamy "smoked" salmon spread can be made far in advance of serving it. Wait until about 1 hour before serving to roll it in the nut mixture. Serve with a variety of crackers or bread rounds.

8 oz. cream cheese, softened
1 can (16 oz.) salmon
2 tsp. minced onion
¼ tsp. Liquid Smoke
1 tbs. lemon juice
1 tbs. horseradish
¼ tsp. salt
1 cup chopped toasted pecans
2 tbs. chopped fresh parsley

With a mixer, beat cream cheese, salmon, minced onion, Liquid Smoke, lemon juice, horseradish and salt until well mixed. Shape mixture into a log. (If mixture is too soft to form into a log, chill for a few minutes before rolling). If not serving immediately, cover log with plastic wrap and refrigerate until ready to serve. Just before serving, mix pecans with parsley. Roll log in pecan-parsley coating and place on a serving platter.

LOW-FAT SALMON MOUSSE

For a pretty presentation, use a mold shaped like a fish or seashell. Surround the unmolded mousse with parsley sprigs and lemon slices. Serve with crackers or bread rounds.

2 pkg. (¼ oz. each) unflavored gelatin
½ cup cold water
1 cup boiling water
¾ cup low-fat or nonfat mayonnaise
2 cans (16 oz. each) salmon, drained
1 tsp. lemon juice
1 tbs. finely minced onion

1 tbs. Worcestershire sauce
1 tsp. salt
¼ tsp. pepper
8 oz. low-fat or nonfat sour cream
fresh parsley sprigs for garnish
lemon slices for garnish

In a small bowl, soak gelatin in cold water until dissolved. Stir in boiling water and cool until thickened. Beat mayonnaise into gelatin mixture until frothy. With a fork, break salmon into pieces, removing any pieces of skin or bones. Add salmon to gelatin mixture with lemon juice, onion, Worcestershire sauce, salt and pepper. Fold in sour cream. Pour mixture into a lightly oiled 6- to 8-cup mold, cover and chill until firm. Invert mold onto a serving platter and garnish with parsley sprigs and lemon slices.

COLD FINGER FOODS

CHUTNEY-STUFFED CELERY

A delightful take on stuffed celery, this low-fat recipe has a spicy, sweet flavor.

1 bunch celery
8 oz. low-fat or nonfat cream
  cheese, softened
1 tsp. white vinegar
1 tsp. curry powder, or more to taste
6 tbs. mango chutney, finely chopped
1-2 tbs. milk
salt and pepper to taste

Separate celery into stalks, remove any tough strands and chill until about 1 hour before serving time. With a mixer, blend remaining ingredients to a thick, but spreadable consistency. Taste and adjust seasonings. Stuff mixture into celery stalks, cut into 2-inch pieces and chill until ready to serve.

STUFFED GRAPE LEAVES

These Greek favorites are otherwise known as dolmades.

1 jar (1 lb.) grape leaves, drained
boiling water
1 cup minced onion
¼ cup chicken stock
1 tsp. salt
1 cup uncooked rice
½ cup pine nuts
½ cup raisins
1 tsp. chopped fresh parsley
½ tsp. dill seeds
3 cloves garlic, minced

1 tsp. dried oregano
1 tsp. ground cumin
½ tsp. ground allspice
1 tsp. dried mint
1 cup hot chicken stock
⅓ cup fresh lemon juice
4 cups warm chicken stock
2 tbs. extra virgin olive oil
1 tsp. salt
sliced lemon wedges for garnish

Wash grape leaves 3 times in cold water to remove excess brine. Soak leaves in boiling water for 1 hour, until pliable. In a skillet, sauté onion for 1 minute to remove excess moisture. Add ¼ cup chicken stock and simmer for 5 minutes. Add 1 tsp. of the salt, rice, pine nuts, raisins, parsley, dill, garlic, oregano, cumin, allspice, mint and 1 cup chicken stock. Cover and simmer for 10 minutes. Stir in ½ of the lemon juice and cool.

Remove thick stem from each grape leaf. Place a layer of grape leaves in a heavy pot and arrange remaining leaves on a work surface, shiny-side down. Place between 1 tsp. and 1 tbs. filling, depending on size of leaves, at the base of each leaf. Fold sides of leaf in over filling and roll up tightly.

Place filled grape leaves in layers in pot. Pour 4 cups chicken stock, remaining lemon juice and oil over rolls and sprinkle with salt. Place a heavy plate on top of rolls to prevent stuffed leaves from unrolling and cover with lid. Cook over low heat for 25 minutes, or until liquid is totally absorbed. Transfer rolls to a serving platter and cool. Garnish with lemon wedges.

BACON-STUFFED CHERRY TOMATOES

Make plenty of these extremely popular appetizers because they will go fast!

2 lb. bacon, finely diced
⅓ cup chopped green onions
½ cup mayonnaise
24 large cherry tomatoes,
    stems removed
lettuce leaves for garnish

In a skillet, cook bacon until browned and crisp. Transfer to paper towels to drain and cool. Crumble bacon and mix in a bowl with green onions and mayonnaise until well blended. Refrigerate until ready to use.

Cut a small a small piece from the bottom of each tomato (opposite the stem end) and scoop out tomato pulp with a melon baller or small spoon. Place hollowed tomatoes hole-side down on paper towels to drain. Fill tomato cavities with bacon mixture and place stem-side down on a serving platter. Surround tomatoes with lettuce and refrigerate until ready to serve.

TUNA-STUFFED EGGS

Here's a new take on deviled eggs. For a colorful variation, add 2 tsp. finely chopped sun-dried tomatoes to the filling. Or, for a more traditional flavor, add 1 tbs. sweet pickle relish.

12 hard-cooked eggs, peeled
1 can (6½ oz.) water-packed tuna,
  drained
¼ cup butter, softened
2 tsp. Dijon mustard
1 tbs. mayonnaise or cream cheese
1 tsp. minced garlic

salt and pepper to taste
dash cayenne pepper
1 tbs. chopped fresh parsley
1 tbs. capers
finely chopped red bell pepper for
  garnish
24 small sprigs parsley for garnish

Slice eggs in half horizontally and place yolks in a small bowl. Cut a sliver from the bottom of each egg white half so that they won't wobble. In a bowl, mash egg yolks finely with a fork. To bowl, add tuna, butter, mustard, mayonnaise, garlic, salt, pepper, cayenne, chopped parsley and capers and mix well. Taste and adjust seasonings. Generously spoon egg yolk mixture into egg white halves. Place on a serving platter and garnish each filled egg with a few pieces of red pepper and a small sprig of parsley.

MARBLEIZED TEA EGGS

Here is a fancy version of deviled eggs. Using vegetables as natural dyes, hard-cooked eggs are steeped in colored water to create a beautiful marbleized pink, green or yellow effect. If desired, garnish each egg with a small piece of parsley and a tiny sliver of red bell pepper. For the beet juice, strain the juice from canned beets.

18 eggs
1 tbs. salt
3 pkg. (10 oz. each) frozen
    chopped spinach
1½ cups water
peels from 4 yellow onions
2½ cups water
2 cups beet juice
½ cup mayonnaise
3 oz. cream cheese
¼ lb. butter, softened
dash Worcestershire sauce
1 tsp. Dijon mustard
salt and white pepper to taste

In a large saucepan, place eggs, 1 tbs. salt and enough cold water to cover eggs by 1 inch. Bring to a boil. Cover, reduce heat to low and cook for 20 minutes. Drain at once and chill in ice water for 5 minutes. Roll eggs gently on a work surface or between your hands until shells are cracked; do not peel.

In a saucepan, combine spinach and 1½ cups water and bring to a boil. Reduce heat to low, cover and simmer for 30 minutes. Strain juice and cool to room temperature. Place 6 eggs in a small, deep bowl and cover with spinach juice. Let stand overnight in the refrigerator.

In another saucepan, combine onion peels and 2½ cups water and bring to a boil. Reduce heat to low and simmer for 20 minutes. Strain juice and cool to room temperature. Place 6 of the eggs in a small, deep bowl and cover with onion juice. Let stand overnight in the refrigerator.

Place remaining 6 eggs in a small, deep bowl and cover with beet juice. Let stand overnight in the refrigerator.

Remove eggs from juices and remove peels. Split eggs in half horizontally and remove yolks. Cut a sliver from the bottom of each egg white half so that they won't wobble. With a food processor or mixer, process yolks with mayonnaise, cream cheese, butter, Worcestershire, mustard, salt and pepper until smooth; taste and adjust seasonings. Place mixture in a pastry bag with a decorative tip and pipe into egg halves. Place filled eggs on a serving platter.

CUCUMBER-HERB CANAPÉS

For this delicate and refreshing appetizer, the cucumbers can be cut into shapes to follow a theme, such as hearts for Valentine's day.

2 large cucumbers (prefer English variety), peeled and cut into ¼-inch slices
1 clove garlic, minced
¼ cup chopped fresh parsley
2 green onions, chopped
8 oz. cream cheese, softened
dash Tabasco Sauce
1 tbs. dry white wine
salt to taste
white pepper to taste
finely minced red bell pepper or 36 small sprigs parsley for garnish

If desired, use a cookie cutter to cut cucumbers slices into shapes. With a food processor or blender, process garlic, parsley and onions until finely minced. Add cream cheese, Tabasco, wine, salt and white pepper and process until well mixed. Taste and adjust seasonings. Transfer ingredients to a pastry bag with a decorative tip and pipe mixture onto cucumber slices. Place on a serving platter, garnish and chill until ready to serve.

CUCUMBER-MINT COOLERS

For your next tea party, serve these light and refreshing cucumber tea sand-wiches.

1 large cucumber, peeled and very thinly sliced
1½ tsp. salt
2½ tbs. chopped fresh mint
½ tsp. sugar
1 tsp. lemon juice
12 tbs. butter, softened
16 slices white bread, crusts removed
pepper to taste
24 sprigs mint for garnish

Place cucumber slices in a colander, sprinkle with salt and let drain for 30 minutes. Pat cucumbers dry on paper towels and set aside. With a food processor or blender, process mint with sugar until finely minced. Add lemon juice and butter and process until smooth. Spread butter mixture on bread slices. Divide cucumbers among ½ of the buttered bread slices and sprinkle with pepper. Cover cucumbers with remaining bread slices, buttered-side down. Cut each sandwich into 3 long strips and serve garnished with mint.

BASIC TEA SANDWICHES

Here is a new twist on an old-fashioned tea party favorite. This recipe works best with a firm variety of pear, such as Bosc. A dense bread, such as potato or egg bread (Challah), makes a firmer sandwich.

PEAR AND CUCUMBER TEA SANDWICHES

8 slices potato, egg or white bread, crusts removed
8 oz. cream cheese, softened
1 cucumber, peeled and thinly sliced
1 firm ripe pear, peeled, if desired, and cored

Spread each bread slice generously with cream cheese. Cover ½ of the bread slices with sliced cucumber and pear, dividing evenly. Cover with remaining bread slices, cheese-side down. Cut each sandwich into 3 strips, place on a serving platter and chill until ready to serve.

VARIATIONS

PEAR, CUCUMBER AND GORGONZOLA TEA SANDWICHES: Mix 1 to 2 oz. crumbled Gorgonzola cheese with cream cheese.

PEAR, CUCUMBER AND MINT TEA SANDWICHES: Mix 1 tbs. chopped fresh mint with cream cheese. If desired, add ½ to 1 tsp. sugar.

PEAR, CUCUMBER AND GOAT CHEESE TEA SANDWICHES: Replace cream cheese with soft goat cheese.

SMOKED CHEESE TEA SANDWICHES WITH CUCUMBER OR PEAR: Use either cucumber or pear and add a thin slice of smoked cheddar cheese. Add a small amount of paprika for color, if desired.

CUCUMBER AND SUN-DRIED TOMATO TEA SANDWICHES: Mix ¼ cup chopped sun-dried tomatoes with cream cheese. Omit pear.

PUMPKIN TEA SANDWICHES

This sweet appetizer is ideal to serve during the fall season. Serve with either **Orange Butter** *or* **Mango Spread**.

1 cup butter, softened
2 tbs. molasses
3 cups sugar
6 large eggs
1 cup orange juice
1 tbs. grated fresh orange peel (zest)
1 can (30 oz.) pumpkin
5 cups all-purpose flour
1 tsp. baking powder
1 tbs. baking soda
¼ tsp. salt
1½ tsp. cinnamon
½ tsp. ground cloves
1½ cups raisins or dried currants
Orange Butter or *Mango Spread*, follow

Heat oven to 350°. Line 3 loaf pans with parchment or brown paper and butter the sides of pan. With a mixer, mix butter, molasses and sugar until light and fluffy. Beat in eggs until mixture is lemon-colored. Add orange juice, orange peel and pumpkin and mix well. In a bowl, mix flour, baking powder, baking soda, salt, cinnamon and cloves and add to pumpkin mixture, mixing well. Stir in raisins. Divide mixture evenly among pans and bake for about 1 hour, or until a knife inserted into the center comes out clean. Cool bread in pans for 10 minutes before transferring to racks to cool. Cut bread into ½-inch slices and cut slices in half. Spread each slice with *Orange Butter* or *Mango Spread* and place open-faced slices in a single layer on a serving platter. Serve at room temperature.

ORANGE BUTTER
Makes ¾ cup

½ cup unsalted butter, softened   ¼ cup orange marmalade

With a food processor or electric mixer, mix butter and marmalade until well blended.

MANGO SPREAD
Makes 1½ cups

8 oz. cream cheese, softened   ½ cup mango chutney

Stir ingredients together until blended.

DATE BREAD WITH PINEAPPLE CREAM CHEESE

Make this bread ahead of time and freeze it. When thawed, cut it into small rectangular shapes and spread with the cream cheese mixture. Garnish the serving platter with colorful edible flowers.

2 cups boiling water
1 lb. chopped pitted dates
2 tbs. butter
2 tsp. baking soda
2 cups sugar
3½ cups all-purpose flour

2 tsp. vanilla extract
1 cup chopped walnuts
8 oz. cream cheese, softened
1 can (10½ oz.) crushed pineapple, drained
sugar to taste, optional

Heat oven to 325°. Line 2 loaf pans with parchment or brown paper and grease well. In a bowl, mix water, dates and butter together; cool. Add baking soda, sugar, flour, vanilla and nuts to bowl, stirring until just mixed. Divide batter evenly among pans and bake for about 1 hour, or until a knife inserted into the center comes out clean. Cool bread in pans for 10 minutes before transferring to racks to cool.

Cut cooled bread into ½-inch slices and cut each slice in half. In a bowl, beat cream cheese with pineapple and sugar, if using. Spread each slice with cream cheese mixture and arrange on a serving platter.

SMOKED TURKEY ROLLS

Serve this fast, easy-to-fix appetizer with honey-mustard dressing for dipping.

1 lb. smoked turkey, sliced
½ lb. cotto salami, thinly sliced
8 oz. cream cheese, softened
½ red bell pepper, thinly sliced
½ yellow bell pepper, thinly sliced
½ green bell pepper, thinly sliced
lettuce leaves

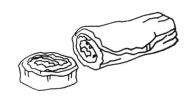

Place a slice of smoked turkey on a piece of plastic wrap. Cover with salami, spread with cream cheese and place 1 strip pepper of each color in center. Roll tightly and chill. Repeat with remaining turkey, salami, cream cheese and peppers. To serve, cut each roll into ½-inch slices and serve on a bed of lettuce.

CHICKEN RELISH SWIRLS

Here's a good way to use leftover chicken. To make clean slices, make sure the rolls are well chilled before cutting.

8 oz. cooked boneless chicken
4 tsp. mango chutney
2 tbs. mayonnaise
1/4 cup chopped green bell pepper
4 green onions, chopped
4 gherkin pickles, chopped

1/4-1/2 tsp. curry powder
salt and pepper to taste
6 slices white bread, crusts removed
1/2 cup butter, softened
about 1 cup stuffed green olives
chopped fresh cilantro for garnish

With a food processor, process chicken until finely minced. Add chutney, mayonnaise, pepper, green onion, pickles, curry powder, salt and pepper and process just until mixed. Taste and adjust seasonings.

With a rolling pin, flatten bread slices and spread with butter. Spread each buttered slice with chicken mixture and arrange a row of olives along the edge of each slice. Roll up bread tightly, jelly-roll style, and wrap securely with plastic wrap. Chill for at least 2 hours. Cut each roll at an angle into 4 slices. Place slices in a single layer on a serving platter and garnish with cilantro.

SMOKED SALMON ROLLS

Viking bread can be found in most grocery stores, usually in the cracker section. It is a large, round cracker bread that is usually rye flavored. You can also use lavosh (Armenian cracker bread). If you can't find cracker bread, thinly slice a round loaf of bread horizontally and remove the crust; it is not necessary to run this under water. Or, use large flour tortillas. If you can't find smoked salmon, add a few drops of liquid smoke to 4 oz. canned salmon.

8 oz. cream cheese, softened
½ cup butter, softened
4 oz. smoked salmon, chopped
2 green onions, chopped
1 pkg. (13 oz.) Viking bread (4 slices per pkg.)

In a bowl, mix softened cream cheese with butter until smooth. Add smoked salmon and green onions and mix until combined. Lightly moisten each slice of Viking bread under running water. Place moistened bread on a work surface. Divide salmon mixture among moistened bread slices, spreading evenly. Roll bread up tightly, wrap securely with plastic wrap and refrigerate for several hours or overnight. Just before serving, remove plastic wrap and cut each roll into 1-inch pieces.

SMOKED SALMON TREATS

These tasty appetizers are relatively quick to fix. If desired, you can substitute 1 can (7¼ oz.) salmon and 4 drops Liquid Smoke for the smoked salmon.

8 oz. cream cheese, softened
8 oz. smoked salmon, chopped
3 tbs. minced green onion
½ loaf sliced white or rye bread, crusts removed
½ cup butter, softened
paprika for garnish

In a bowl, mix cream cheese with salmon and green onion until well mixed. On a work surface, flatten bread with a rolling pin. Spread butter over half of the slices on one side. With a fluted round 2-inch cutter, cut 2 circles from each slice of bread. Spread salmon mixture on buttered bread shapes and place on a platter. Spread remaining bread slices with butter on both sides and cut into shapes with cutter. Cover each salmon-covered slice with buttered slices, lining up the edges. Press halves lightly together, sprinkle each buttered top with paprika and chill until ready to serve.

ANCHOVY BUTTER ROUNDS

The exotic, salty and pungent flavor of anchovies is appreciated by those with discerning taste buds. Capers are the small buds of plants that grow along the Mediterranean and come packed in a salty brine. They add a lively flavor to recipes.

10 anchovies
½ cup butter, softened
24 small toasted bread rounds
2-3 tbs. small capers

In a bowl, mash anchovies and mix thoroughly with butter. Chill for at least 1 hour. Spread toasted bread rounds with anchovy butter, sprinkle with capers and place on a serving platter.

SHRIMP SALAD PUFFS

These little cream puffs are filled with a subtly flavored shrimp salad mixture. Be sure to beat the cream puff batter very well. The beating action develops the gluten in the flour, which helps the puffs to rise high. Don't fill the puffs until just before serving or they will get soggy.

½ cup butter
pinch salt
1 cup water
1 cup all-purpose flour
4 eggs
3 oz. cream cheese, softened
1 jar (4 oz.) olive pimiento cheese spread
½ cup purchased blue cheese salad dressing
½ cup mayonnaise
2 tbs. ketchup
¼ tsp. Worcestershire sauce
¼ tsp. prepared horseradish
1 tbs. lemon juice, or to taste
1 clove garlic, minced
1 can (6 oz.) shrimp

Heat oven to 400°. In a saucepan, bring butter, salt and water to a boil; remove from heat. Add flour to pan all at once and stir until dough comes together in a ball and leaves the sides of pan. Cool dough slightly. Add eggs to dough, one at a time, beating very vigorously until a smooth batter is formed. Drop batter by teaspoonfuls onto a greased baking sheet. Bake for 10 minutes, reduce oven heat to 350° and bake for 20 minutes. Remove puffs from oven and place on wire racks to cool.

Process remaining ingredients, except shrimp, with a food processor or blender until well mixed. Transfer to a bowl and stir in shrimp.

To serve, split cooled puffs in half, fill with shrimp mixture and place on a serving platter.

PASTA SHELLS FILLED WITH SHRIMP AND VEGETABLES

Stuffed pasta shells are a quick, substantial appetizer that can be made ahead of time. For a luncheon entrée, serve several of these on each plate.

½ cup chopped water chestnuts
2 cups chopped celery
2 cups grated carrots
¼-½ cup chopped green onions
2 cups cooked baby shrimp
2 cups shredded regular or low-fat
    sharp cheddar cheese

1 cup regular or low-fat mayonnaise
1 tbs. lemon juice, or to taste
1 tsp. sugar
1 lb. jumbo pasta shells, cooked,
    drained and cooled
lettuce leaves

In a bowl, mix water chestnuts, celery, carrots, green onions, shrimp and cheddar cheese until well mixed. In a separate bowl, mix mayonnaise, lemon juice and sugar until blended; stir into shrimp mixture. Fill pasta shells with shrimp mixture and chill until ready to serve. Line a serving platter with lettuce leaves and arrange stuffed shells on top.

STRAWBERRIES STUFFED WITH ORANGE CREAM CHEESE

Refresh your guests with this sweet appetizer. Or, use this recipe as a light dessert. If desired, surround the fruit with attractive greenery, such as fresh mint, watercress or well-cleaned greens from the garden. Use Grand Marnier, Curaçao or Triple Sec for the liqueur.

1 pt. strawberries
8 oz. cream cheese, softened
confectioners' sugar to taste
orange-flavored liqueur to taste

Remove stems from berries to create a flat surface so that berries stand with their points facing up. With a small knife, cut an X through the pointed end of each berry, ¼ of the way down. Place berries on their bases on a serving dish. With a mixer or food processor, process cream cheese with sugar and liqueur until well blended. Place mixture into a pastry bag with a star tip. Pipe cream cheese mixture into the center of each berry. Serve immediately.

FRUIT KABOBS

Fruit makes a refreshing appetizer that is ideal to serve during the summer months. Kids especially love this one.

3 bananas, peeled
3 apples
2 tbs. lemon juice mixed with 1 cup
   cold water
3 kiwi fruits, peeled and cut into chunks

2 oranges, peeled and sectioned
1 cantaloupe, honeydew, watermelon or
   other melon, rind removed and cut
   into cubes
1 cup fresh or canned pineapple chunks

DIPPING SAUCES

nonfat sour cream mixed with orange juice and honey to taste, optional
low-fat or nonfat flavored yogurt, optional
plain yogurt flavored with extracts to taste, optional

granola for coating, optional

Cut bananas into chunks. Core apples, peel if desired and cut into large chunks. Dip bananas and apples in lemon juice mixture to prevent darkening. Thread prepared fruits on wooden skewers, alternating types. Refrigerate until ready to serve. Serve with your choice of dipping sauces and granola, if desired.

CREAMY STUFFED DATES

Garnish this quick and easy recipe with twisted orange slices and a few mint sprigs.

40 whole pitted dates
8 oz. regular, low-fat or nonfat cream cheese, softened
⅓ cup orange liqueur
sugar to taste, optional
2 tbs. grated fresh orange peel (zest)

Cut dates in half lengthwise and place cut-side up on a serving platter. In a bowl, mix cream cheese with orange liqueur and sugar. Place cream cheese mixture in a pastry bag with a decorative tip and pipe into date halves. Sprinkle with grated orange peel.

HOT FINGER FOODS

WARM CHEESE WAFERS

This is a great recipe to keep frozen and ready to bake when drop-in guests come a-calling.

½ cup butter, cut into pieces
½ lb. Brie cheese, rind removed and cubed, or
    ½ lb. sharp cheddar cheese, shredded
1 cup flour
¼ tsp. seasoned salt
½ tsp. Tabasco Sauce
¼ cup sesame seeds

With a food processor or mixer, process butter and cheese until well blended. Add flour, seasoned salt and Tabasco and mix until a smooth dough forms. Divide dough into 4 equal pieces and shape each piece into a 1-inch-diameter log. Wrap logs with waxed paper and refrigerate or freeze until ready to serve.

Heat oven to 400°. Cut each log into ¼-inch slices. Place slices 1 inch apart on ungreased baking sheets and sprinkle with sesame seeds. Bake for 8 to 10 minutes or until edges are golden brown. Cool slightly and serve immediately.

FRIED CHEESE SQUARES

This favorite Greek appetizer is typically served with retsina wine and crusty bread. Look for the cheeses in a Greek deli or specialty store.

½ lb. Kefalotyri, kasseri, Asiago or
   Romano cheese
¼ cup olive oil
¼ cup butter
3 large eggs, beaten with a little water
1 cup flour for dredging

2 tbs. brandy
2 tbs. lemon juice
¼ tsp. dried oregano
chopped fresh parsley
lemon wedges for garnish

Heat oven to 400°. Place an ovenproof dish in oven to heat. Cut cheese into 12 ¼-inch-thick squares or triangles. In a deep-sided skillet, heat oil and butter over medium heat. Dip cheese squares in beaten eggs and dredge in flour. Carefully place coated cheese in skillet and fry until golden brown on both sides. Transfer fried cheese to heated ovenproof dish.

In a small saucepan, heat brandy until just below the boiling point and immediately pour over cheese. Carefully tilt dish and ignite hot brandy with a match. When flames have died down, sprinkle with lemon juice, oregano and parsley. Serve immediately, garnished with lemon wedges.

FRENCH CAVIAR POTATOES

For this simple and sophisticated presentation, arrange potatoes on a bed of shredded lettuce or fresh parsley. If desired, use 2 colors of caviar for eye appeal and variety.

60 tiny new potatoes,
    cooked until tender
oil for deep frying
8 oz. sour cream
1 jar (2 oz.) caviar,
    rinsed and drained

Heat oven to 200°. Slice a small piece from the bottom of each potato so that they won't wobble. With a melon baller or small spoon, scoop out the centers of potatoes; reserve centers for another use or discard. Heat oil in a deep fryer or deep pan to 375°. Carefully drop prepared potatoes into hot oil and fry until crisp. Remove potatoes with a strainer and drain on paper towels; keep warm on a baking sheet in a 200° oven until ready to serve. Just before serving, fill warm potatoes with sour cream and top with a small amount of caviar. Serve immediately.

MINIATURE FRENCH QUICHES

Makes 32

These are best served slightly warm, but they can also be served at room temperature. For ease, assemble this recipe ahead of time and freeze. Thaw quiches for 2 to 3 hours in the refrigerator before baking.

2 cups all-purpose flour
pinch salt
6 oz. cold butter, cut into pieces
⅓ cup cold water
8 slices bacon, finely diced
1 medium onion, diced
4 large eggs, beaten
1 cup milk
1 cup heavy cream
¼ tsp. nutmeg
½ tsp. salt
¼ tsp. pepper
¼ cup chopped green chiles, optional
¼ cup shredded Swiss cheese
¼ cup shredded cheddar cheese

With a food processor, process flour, salt and butter just until crumbly. Add water and process until dough just holds together; take care not to overmix. Remove dough, wrap with plastic wrap and refrigerate for 30 minutes. On a lightly floured work surface, roll dough until ⅛-inch thick. With a 2½-inch round fluted cutter, cut dough into 32 rounds. Line miniature muffin tins with pastry dough and chill until ready to fill.

Heat oven to 450°. In a skillet, fry bacon pieces over medium-high heat until crisp and drain on paper towels. Add onion to skillet with bacon fat and sauté over medium heat until wilted. In a bowl, mix eggs, milk, cream, nutmeg, salt and pepper until blended. Distribute bacon, onion, chiles and cheeses evenly among pastry shells. Pour egg mixture into pastry shells, dividing evenly. Bake for 10 minutes. Reduce oven heat to 350° and bake for about 8 minutes, until eggs are set.

SHRIMP TARTLETS

Serve these simple, creamy quiche-like tarts slightly warm or at room temperature.

1 cup plus 2 tbs. all-purpose flour
½ cup butter, cut into pieces
1 tbs. grated Parmesan cheese
1 egg, slightly beaten
dash salt
8 oz. cream cheese, softened

1 tbs. milk
1 tsp. Worcestershire sauce
1 green onion, minced
¼ cup purchased chili sauce
½ lb. small cooked shrimp
chopped fresh parsley for garnish

With a food processor or blender, process flour, butter, Parmesan, egg and salt until dough is well mixed. Wrap dough in plastic and chill for 30 minutes.

Heat oven to 425°. Divide dough into 18 equal balls and press each ball into a miniature muffin cup or small tart pan. With a food processor or blender, mix cream cheese, milk, Worcestershire sauce and green onion until smooth. Pour mixture into pastry shells, dividing evenly. Top each tartlet with a small amount of chili sauce and a few shrimp; sprinkle with parsley. Bake for 10 minutes, or until set. Remove from oven and place on a rack to cool.

QUESADILLAS

*Serve this cheesy Mexican-style delight with **Guacamole**, page 28, and sour cream for dipping. Be sure to provide lots of napkins!*

4 oz. sharp cheddar cheese, shredded
4 oz. Monterey Jack cheese, shredded
vegetable oil for frying
twelve 8-inch flour tortillas
4 green onions, chopped
1 can (4 oz.) diced green chiles

Heat oven to 200°. Mix cheeses together. In a medium skillet, add enough oil to coat bottom of pan and heat over medium heat. Place 1 tortilla in pan. Sprinkle with ⅙ each of the cheese, green onions and diced chiles. Cover with another tortilla. When tortilla is golden brown, flip quesadilla over with a spatula. Cook until opposite side is golden brown and cheese is melted. Transfer quesadilla to a paper towel-lined baking sheet and keep warm in oven. Repeat cooking process with remaining ingredients, adding a layer of paper towels between each layer of quesadillas. To serve, cut each quesadilla into 6 wedges and serve immediately.

RED ONION FOCACCIA

You'll love the delicious cooked onion topping on this well-loved Italian flat-bread. Make it on a pizza pan and cut it into small squares or wedges. For ease, you can make the dough with a bread machine, using the dough cycle.

2 tsp. active dry yeast
pinch sugar
1 cup warm water
2½ cups all-purpose flour
½ tsp. salt
1 tbs. olive oil
1¾ lb. red onions, thinly sliced
⅓ cup olive oil
1 tsp. anchovy paste
1 tbs. white vinegar
olive oil for brushing
salt and pepper to taste

In a bowl, dissolve yeast and sugar in warm water. Add about 1 cup of the flour and beat vigorously for 1 minute. Let mixture rise in a warm, draft-free place until doubled in bulk, about 30 minutes. Punch mixture down and add salt, 1 tbs. oil and remaining flour, a little at a time, until dough comes together in a ball and is not too sticky. On a floured work surface, knead dough well for about 10 minutes. Let dough rest for 15 minutes.

In a skillet over low heat, cook onions in $\frac{1}{3}$ cup olive oil until softened. Dissolve anchovy paste in vinegar and add to skillet with onions. Cook over medium heat until onions are soft and liquid has evaporated, about 5 minutes. Cool.

Punch down dough and shape to fit a 12-inch pizza pan. Let rise in a warm, draft-free place for 30 minutes. Heat oven to 400°. Brush dough lightly with olive oil and sprinkle with salt and pepper. Taste onions, adjusting seasonings if necessary, and spread gently on dough within $\frac{1}{2}$-inch of edge. Bake in a 400° oven for 30 to 35 minutes until lightly browned. To serve, cut into small squares with a pizza cutter or large knife.

MUSHROOM STRUDEL TARTS

Phyllo dough-lined muffin tins feature a wonderful mushroom and onion filling. Try this recipe with different varieties of mushrooms for a delightful change.

4 sheets phyllo dough, thawed if frozen
6 tbs. *Clarified Butter*, page 139
1 lb. white or brown mushrooms, chopped
½ cup chopped onion

¼ cup chopped fresh parsley
½ cup dry white wine
dash Tabasco Sauce
4 oz. Monterey Jack cheese, shredded

Heat oven to 400°. Place 1 sheet of the phyllo on a work surface and brush with *Clarified Butter*. Cover with another phyllo sheet and brush again with butter. Repeat layering and brushing with remaining phyllo. Cut phyllo stack into 24 squares and place each square in miniature muffin cup.

In a skillet over medium-high heat, sauté mushrooms with onion, parsley, wine and Tabasco until liquid is almost evaporated; cool. Fill muffin cups with mushroom mixture and top with cheese, dividing evenly. Bake for 15 to 18 minutes, until phyllo is golden brown and filling is hot. Keep warm in a chafing dish, or in a baking dish set on an electric warming tray.

HERBED MUSHROOM CAPS

This is a great recipe to prepare ahead of time: Add all ingredients to the skillet, remove the pan from heat and refrigerate the mixture, covered, for up to 2 days before continuing the cooking process.

3 lb. white or brown mushrooms
½ cup chicken stock
1 large onion, finely chopped
2 tsp. dried basil
2 tsp. dried oregano
½ tsp. dried thyme

2 cloves garlic, minced
dash Tabasco Sauce
½ cup dry sherry
¼ cup lemon juice
salt to taste

Cut stems from mushrooms at base of caps; reserve stems for another use or discard. In a skillet over medium heat, heat chicken stock until bubbling. Add onion and mushrooms and cook until limp. Add remaining ingredients and cook uncovered until liquid is reduced to ½ cup, stirring occasionally. Serve hot in a chafing dish, or in a baking dish set on an electric warming tray.

PESTO MUSHROOMS

These whip together in minutes. For another variation, use chive-flavored cream cheese and crumbled bacon instead of pesto.

2 tbs. butter
1 clove garlic, minced
16 large white or brown mushrooms
salt and pepper to taste
4 oz. cream cheese, softened
⅓ cup purchased pesto

In a small saucepan, melt butter over medium heat and sauté garlic until soft, but not browned. Cut stems from mushrooms at base of caps. Reserve mushroom stems for another use or discard. Brush mushroom caps with garlic butter mixture and place cap-side down in an ovenproof dish. Sprinkle caps with salt and pepper. Mix cream cheese with pesto until blended and mound mixture in the center of each cap, dividing evenly. Refrigerate for several hours or overnight.

When ready to serve, heat oven to 400°. Bake mushrooms for 5 to 6 minutes or until filling is soft and mushrooms are warm. Serve hot in a chafing dish, or in a baking dish set on an electric warming tray.

PATÉ MUSHROOMS

Paté is available in a variety of flavors and textures in many grocery stores and specialty food stores. Experiment with your favorite type of paté for this simple, fast recipe.

60 medium white or brown mushrooms
¼ lb. paté, mashed with a fork
finely chopped fresh parsley for garnish

Heat broiler. Cut stems from mushrooms at base of caps. Reserve mushroom stems for another use or discard. Place mushrooms cap-side down on a baking sheet and fill each cap with a small mound of paté. Broil for 2 to 3 minutes, until piping hot. Garnish with parsley. Serve hot in a chafing dish, or in a baking dish set on an electric warming tray.

SPINACH-STUFFED MUSHROOMS

Squeeze the spinach very dry. Otherwise, the filling leaches too much liquid and the appetizer is too messy to handle.

2 tbs. butter
¼ cup minced onion
1 cup chopped frozen spinach, thawed and squeezed very dry
½ cup low-fat ricotta cheese
¼ cup grated Parmesan cheese
salt and pepper to taste
nutmeg to taste
1 lb. medium white or brown mushrooms

Heat oven to 350°. In a skillet, heat butter over medium heat and sauté onion until limp. Add spinach, ricotta cheese, Parmesan cheese, salt, pepper and nutmeg; taste and adjust seasonings. Cut stems from mushrooms at base of caps. Reserve mushroom stems for another use or discard. Place mushrooms cap-side down on a baking sheet and fill each cap with a small mound of filling. Bake for about 20 minutes. Serve hot in a chafing dish, or in a baking dish set on an electric warming tray.

HAWAIIAN-STYLE STUFFED MUSHROOMS

This rich, creamy appetizer is elegant enough to use as a starter for a fancy meal. Serve it with crusty rolls. To set the ambiance, use exotic Hawaiian flowers as a centerpiece for the table or buffet.

¼ cup butter
3 large sweet onions, thinly sliced
16 extra-large white or brown
   mushrooms
4 oz. fresh crabmeat

1 green onion, finely chopped
3 oz. cream cheese
salt and pepper to taste
¼ lb. Monterey Jack cheese, shredded

Heat oven to 350°. In a skillet, melt butter over medium-high heat and sauté onions until golden brown. Transfer onions to a casserole, or divide among 8 individual ramekins. Cut stems from mushrooms at base of caps. Reserve mushroom stems for another use or discard. Place mushrooms cap-side up in casserole or ramekins on top of onions. Mix together crabmeat, green onion, cream cheese, salt and pepper. Fill each mushroom cap with a small mound of crabmeat mixture. Bake for 5 to 8 minutes or until mushrooms are softened. Sprinkle with Monterey Jack and continue to bake until cheese melts. Serve hot in a chafing dish, or in a baking dish set on an electric warming tray.

CRAB-STUFFED MUSHROOMS

Servings: 8

This chic appetizer is delicately flavored and rich. As a starter for a meal, limit the quantity to 2 stuffed mushrooms per person.

8 oz. cream cheese, softened
½ lb. crabmeat
1½ cup fine seasoned breadcrumbs
1 clove garlic, finely minced
16 extra-large white or brown mushrooms
2 tbs. grated Parmesan cheese
paprika for garnish

Heat broiler. With a mixer, beat cream cheese until soft. Gently stir in crabmeat, breadcrumbs and garlic. Cut stems from mushrooms at base of caps. Reserve mushroom stems for another use or discard. Place mushrooms cap-side down on a baking sheet and fill each mushroom cap with a small mound of crabmeat mixture. Sprinkle with Parmesan and paprika. Broil until piping hot, about 5 minutes. Serve hot in a chafing dish, or in a baking dish set on an electric warming tray.

CHEESY CRAB TOAST

This recipe is very simple, but it tastes complicated. In a pinch, imitation crab-meat can be substituted for crabmeat.

4 French rolls
½ cup butter, melted
6-8 tsp. Dijon mustard
12 oz. crabmeat
8 oz. sharp cheddar cheese, shredded
2 tbs. minced fresh parsley
paprika for garnish

Heat broiler. Cut rolls in half lengthwise and brush with melted butter. Place rolls on a baking sheet buttered-side up and toast under broiler until golden brown. Remove rolls from oven and spread each half with mustard. Evenly distribute crab-meat among roll halves and sprinkle with cheese. Broil until cheese melts. Remove from oven and sprinkle with parsley and paprika. Cut rolls into 1-inch diagonal slices. Serve hot in a chafing dish, or in a baking dish set on an electric warming tray.

ASIAN SHRIMP TOAST

This popular appetizer should be fried just before the guests arrive. Or, provide a fondue pot filled with hot oil and let the guests to cook their own treats.

8 slices white bread, square loaf, crusts removed
1 lb. uncooked shrimp, peeled and deveined
½ cups finely minced onion
½ tsp. minced fresh ginger
1 tsp. salt
2 tsp. cornstarch
1 egg
sesame seeds for coating, optional
oil for deep frying

Cut each bread slice into 4 triangles and let dry for 1 to 2 hours. Heat oven to 200°. Chop shrimp finely and place in a bowl. Add onion, ginger, salt, cornstarch and egg and mix into a smooth paste. Spread shrimp paste on bread triangles. If desired, dip bread triangles in sesame seeds. In a deep saucepan, wok or fondue pot, heat oil to 350°. Fry bread triangles until both sides are golden brown. Drain on paper towels. Serve hot in a chafing dish, or in a baking dish set on an electric warming tray.

GRILLED MARINATED SHRIMP

This very simple, tasteful appetizer wows your guests. If a barbecue is not available, the prawns can be quickly sautéed in the marinade mixture. Provide a small dish for the guests to place the shrimp tails after eating.

1 lb. large shrimp (18-24 per lb.)
1 cup olive oil
2 cloves garlic, minced
1 tsp. salt
½ tsp. chili powder
1 tbs. chopped fresh parsley

Peel shrimp, leaving tails intact. Mix remaining ingredients together and pour over shrimp in a baking dish. Let stand for 1 hour. Prepare a medium-hot barbecue fire or heat grill to high. Grill shrimp, basting with marinade, for about 3 minutes on each side, until shrimp turn pink; take care not to overcook. Serve hot in a chafing dish, or in a baking dish set on an electric warming tray.

BACON-WRAPPED SCALLOPS
WITH BÉARNAISE SAUCE

These crispy tidbits are dipped in a Béarnaise sauce that can be made in minutes with a food processor or blender.

1 lb. sliced bacon, cut into thirds
1 lb. scallops, muscles removed
3 egg yolks
6 oz. butter, melted, kept warm
salt and pepper to taste

1 tbs. lemon juice, or more to taste
1 tbs. white wine vinegar
1 shallot, minced
1 tsp. mixed fresh tarragon, chervil and
   parsley

Heat broiler. In a large pot of boiling water, cook bacon pieces for about 5 minutes; drain and cool. Wrap each scallop with a piece of bacon, secure with a toothpick and place on a broiler pan. Broil until nicely browned; keep warm.

With a food processor or blender, process yolks until light yellow in color. With machine running, slowly add warm melted butter in a thin stream. Add salt, pepper, lemon juice, vinegar, shallot and herbs and process until mixed. Taste and adjust seasonings and lemon juice.

Serve scallops hot in a chafing dish, or in a baking dish set on an electric warming tray. Serve sauce in a dish on the side.

BAKED CLAMS

For a dramatic presentation, arrange the clams on the half-shell on an oven-proof serving platter that is covered with rock salt. Provide a small dish for the discarded shells.

40 clams, well scrubbed
¼ cup water
rock salt, optional
½ cup finely chopped fresh Italian
   parsley

4 cloves garlic, minced
½ cup dried breadcrumbs
¼ cup olive oil or chicken stock
½ tsp. dried oregano
salt and pepper to taste

Place clams in a saucepan with water. Bring water to a boil over medium-high heat, cover pan tightly and steam just until clam shells open, about 2 minutes. Drain and discard any unopened shells. Snap off each top shell from clams and discard.

Heat broiler. Cover an ovenproof serving platter with a layer of rock salt, if desired, and arrange clam shells decoratively on platter. Mix remaining ingredients together, taste and adjust seasonings. Place a small amount of parsley mixture over each clam and broil until heated through and browned. Serve immediately.

TERIYAKI CHICKEN SKEWERS

Make this great recipe ahead of time — it takes just minutes to broil when the guests arrive.

3½ lb. boneless chicken breasts
¼ cup soy sauce
1 tbs. molasses
1½ cups dry white wine
1 cup water
2 tsp. salt
2 tsp. pepper
2 tsp. minced garlic
1 medium onion, minced
shredded lettuce
Brandied Mayonnaise, follows, optional

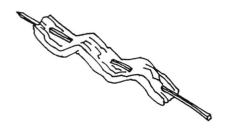

Cut chicken breasts into thin strips, thread onto wooden skewers and place in a shallow pan. In a bowl, combine soy sauce, molasses, wine, water, salt, pepper, garlic, and onion and pour over chicken strips. Cover pan and refrigerate overnight.

Heat broiler. Broil chicken pieces for about 3 minutes on each side, until cooked through. Serve on a bed of shredded lettuce alone or with a bowl of *Brandied Mayonnaise*.

BRANDIED MAYONNAISE
Makes 1 cup

This makes a delightful change from the ordinary dipping sauce.

¾ cup purchased mayonnaise
1 tbs. brandy
3 tbs. ketchup
1 tbs. Worcestershire sauce
1 tbs. honey
1 tbs. lemon juice
salt and pepper to taste

Blend all ingredients, taste and adjust seasonings. Cover and chill until ready to serve.

SESAME-WALNUT CHICKEN STRIPS

*Using ground roasted Szechwan peppercorns creates a unique, fragrant taste sensation. Look for roasted Szechwan pepper in the international section of the supermarket or in an Asian market. If desired, serve these with homemade **Sweet and Sour Sauce**.*

8 boneless, skinless chicken breast
   halves
2 cups walnuts
2 cups sesame seeds
oil for deep frying

salt to taste
ground roasted Szechwan pepper or
   black pepper to taste
Sweet and Sour Sauce, follows, optional

Heat oven to 200°. Cut each chicken breast half into 5 long strips. With a food processor or blender, process walnuts with sesame seeds until finely ground and place in a shallow dish. In a deep pot, wok or fondue pot, heat oil to 350°. Dip chicken pieces into nut mixture and drop into hot oil. Fry for several minutes, turning once, until golden brown and cooked through. Remove chicken from oil, drain on paper towels and sprinkle with salt and pepper. Keep warm in oven until ready to serve. Cut strips into small diagonal pieces. Serve hot in a chafing dish, or in a baking dish set on an electric warming tray. Serve *Sweet and Sour Sauce*, if using, in a bowl on the side.

SWEET AND SOUR SAUCE

Here's an easy, tasty version of sweet and sour sauce.

¾ cup pineapple juice
½ tbs. cornstarch
½ cup brown sugar, firmly packed
1 tsp. salt
½ cup cider vinegar
¼ cup ketchup
1 cup crushed pineapple, drained
few drops red food coloring, optional

In a saucepan, mix pineapple juice with cornstarch. Add remaining ingredients and bring to a boil over medium-high heat, stirring constantly, until mixture thickens. Remove from heat. Serve warm or at room temperature.

TERIYAKI CHICKEN WINGS

These will disappear fast when serving a crowd, so be sure to make plenty. Keep them warm in a chafing dish and provide lots of napkins.

2 lb. chicken wings
1 small onion, chopped
½ cup soy sauce
½ cup brown sugar, firmly packed
1 tsp. minced fresh ginger
2 cloves garlic, minced
2 tbs. dry sherry
sesame seeds for garnish, optional

Heat oven to 350°. With a knife, separate chicken wings at the joints and discard tips. Place wing pieces in a baking dish. With a food processor or blender, process onion, soy sauce, brown sugar, ginger, garlic and sherry until blended. Pour mixture over chicken and marinate for at least 1 hour. Bake for 1 hour and sprinkle with sesame seeds, if using. Serve hot in a chafing dish, or in a baking dish set on an electric warming tray.

BARBECUE CHICKEN WINGS

This is a great recipe for traveling, because you can simply unplug the crockery pot and transport it to the party. To help your host, consider bringing an extension cord so the crockery pot can be easily placed. Remember to provide lots of napkins.

4 lb. chicken wings
2 large onions, chopped
2 cans (6 oz. each) tomato paste
2 large cloves garlic, minced
¼ cup Worcestershire sauce
¼ cup cider vinegar

½ cup brown sugar
½ cup sweet pickle relish
½ cup red or white wine
2 tsp. salt
2 tsp. dry mustard

With a knife, separate chicken wings at the joints and discard tips. Place wing pieces in a crockery pot or other slow cooker. Add remaining ingredients to pot and stir well. Set crockery pot on LOW and cook for 5 to 6 hours. Serve directly from crockery pot, in a chafing dish, or in a baking dish set on an electric warming tray.

HONEY CHICKEN WINGS

Chicken wings are fashionable fare for casual get-togethers. Make plenty of these — and don't forget the napkins.

3 lb. chicken wings
salt and pepper to taste
1 cup honey
3 tbs. ketchup
½ cup soy sauce
2 tbs. vegetable oil
1 clove garlic, minced
sesame seeds for garnish, optional

Heat oven to 350°. With a knife, separate chicken wings at the joints and discard tips. Place wing pieces in a shallow baking dish and sprinkle with salt and pepper. Mix together remaining ingredients, except sesame seeds, and pour mixture over chicken. Bake for 50 minutes. Sprinkle with sesame seeds, if using. Serve hot in a chafing dish, or in a baking dish set on an electric warming tray.

TURKEY MEATBALLS

Serve these savory meatballs plain or submerged in your favorite sauce. A delicate sour cream sauce is especially nice.

1 lb. ground turkey
2 tbs. mayonnaise
2 tbs. minced onion
salt and pepper to taste
seasoned flour for dipping

Heat oven to 350°. In a bowl, mix turkey with mayonnaise, onion, salt and pepper. Shape mixture into 36 small balls, roll balls in seasoned flour and place on a broiler pan. Bake for about 20 minutes, or until cooked through. Serve hot in a chafing dish, or in a baking dish set on an electric warming tray. Provide toothpicks for serving.

SWEET AND SOUR MEATBALLS

You can make these into a meal for 4 to 6 people by serving them over rice.

½ cup fresh breadcrumbs
½ cup milk
1 lb. lean ground beef
¼ cup chopped onion
1½ tsp. salt
¼ tsp. pepper
2 eggs, beaten
½ cup flour
2 tbs. butter

1¼ cups cold water
1 tbs. cornstarch
¼ cup sugar
¼ cup vinegar
1 tbs. soy sauce
½ tsp. salt
⅓ cup sliced green and/or red bell
   peppers

In a bowl, combine breadcrumbs and milk and let stand for 5 minutes. Add beef, onion, 1½ tsp. salt and pepper and blend well. Shape mixture into 32 balls. Dip balls in beaten egg and roll in flour. In a large skillet, heat butter over medium-high heat. Add meatballs to skillet and brown on all sides. In a saucepan, combine water and cornstarch and stir until dissolved. Add sugar, vinegar, soy sauce and ½ tsp. salt. Add browned meatballs and cook over medium heat until mixture thickens. Add peppers, cover and simmer for 10 minutes. Serve hot in a chafing dish, or in a baking dish set on an electric warming tray. Provide toothpicks for serving.

ITALIAN-STYLE MEATBALLS

This Northern-Italian version of meatballs can be served with your favorite Italian meat or tomato sauce. Or, for an American version, try barbecue sauce.

1 slice bread, soaked in milk
1 lb. ground beef chuck
¼ cup grated Parmesan cheese
¼ cup minced onion
2 cloves garlic, minced
1 tbs. grated fresh lemon peel (zest)

¼ cup minced fresh parsley
1 egg, beaten
salt and pepper to taste
oil for sautéing
about 4 cups tomato, meat or
    barbecue sauce

Heat broiler. Squeeze milk from bread and place bread in a large bowl with ground beef, Parmesan, onion, garlic, lemon peel, parsley, egg, salt and pepper; mix until well blended. In a skillet, heat a small amount of oil over medium-high heat. Cook a small amount of meat mixture in oil until done, taste and adjust seasonings. Shape meat mixture into 24 small balls and place on a broiler pan. Broil meatballs until browned on all sides. Transfer to a large skillet with sauce and simmer for about 1 hour, until cooked through. Serve hot in a chafing dish, or in a baking dish set on an electric warming tray. Provide toothpicks for serving.

PORK AND PINEAPPLE SKEWERS

Plum sauce is a perfect partner for pork, but it also works well with beef or chicken. If time is limited, look for prepared plum sauce in the international section of the grocery store. Soak bamboo skewers in water for about 30 minutes before using so they won't burn while grilling.

6 cloves garlic, minced
1 tbs. ground coriander
1 tbs. turmeric
1 tbs. brown sugar
1 tbs. ground cumin
1 tsp. white pepper

1 tsp. salt
½ cup coconut milk
2 lb. pork tenderloin, thinly sliced
fresh pineapple, cut into ½-inch
   wedges
Plum Sauce, follows

In a shallow dish, mix garlic, coriander, turmeric, brown sugar, cumin, white pepper, salt and coconut milk until blended. Add pork slices. Cover dish and refrigerate for several hours or overnight.

Heat broiler or grill to high. Thread pork lengthwise onto soaked wooden skewers and thread a pineapple slice at the end of each skewer. Grill or broil until cooked through, about 3 minutes per side. Serve hot in a chafing dish, or in a baking dish set on an electric warming tray. Serve *Plum Sauce* in a bowl on the side.

PLUM SAUCE

The secret ingredient in this quick plum sauce is Chinese five-spice powder, which can be found in many grocery stores or Asian markets.

2 cups plum preserves
¼ cup unseasoned rice vinegar
2 tsp. Chinese five-spice powder
1 tbs. instant chicken bouillon granules
1 tbs. soy sauce

In a microwavable bowl, mix all ingredients. Microwave on HIGH for 3 minutes. Stir well and cook for 1 minute. Cool and store in the refrigerator until ready to use.

Or, stir all ingredients together in a medium saucepan. Heat over medium heat for 8 to 10 minutes, stirring occasionally, until mixture thickens slightly. Cool and store in the refrigerator until ready to use.

HOISIN SPARERIBS

Servings: 8-12

If you have trouble finding some of these ingredients, look in the international section of the supermarket or in an Asian market. Ask your butcher to cut the ribs crosswise into 1½-inch strips.

3 lb. pork spareribs, cut into 1½-inch strips
2 cloves garlic, minced
½ tsp. minced fresh ginger
3 tbs. hoisin sauce
2 tbs. sugar
¼ cup soy sauce
¼ cup dry sherry
¼ tsp. Chinese five-spice powder
½ cup water

Place ribs in a foil-lined shallow baking pan. Mix remaining ingredients together, except water, and pour over ribs. Marinate for 1 hour.

Heat oven to 300°. Add water to pan and cover with foil. Bake ribs for 2½ to 3 hours. Serve hot in a chafing dish, or in a baking dish set on an electric warming tray.

SWEET AND SOUR PUPUS

Pupu is the Hawaiian word for appetizer. This favorite can be made ahead of time and baked just before the guests arrive. Scallops or cooked chicken livers can be substituted for the water chestnuts.

1 lb. bacon, cut into thirds
2 cans (4 oz. each) whole water
    chestnuts
¾ cup pineapple juice
1½ tbs. cornstarch
½ cup brown sugar, firmly packed

½ cup cider vinegar
1 tsp. salt
4 tsp. ketchup
1 cup crushed pineapple, drained
few drops red food coloring, optional

Heat oven to 350°. In a large pot of boiling water, cook bacon pieces for about 5 minutes; drain and cool. Wrap 1 piece of bacon around each water chestnut, secure with a toothpick and place in an ovenproof dish. In a saucepan, mix pineapple juice with cornstarch and bring to a boil. Add remaining ingredients and cook, stirring, until mixture is slightly thickened. Pour sauce over bacon-wrapped water chestnuts. Bake for 30 minutes until heated through. Serve hot in a chafing dish, or in a baking dish set on an electric warming tray.

WRAPPED DELICACIES

THREE-CHEESE PHYLLO WITH WALNUTS

Wine tasting? Choose this delicate appetizer for a perfect accompaniment. While working with phyllo, keep it covered with a slightly damp cloth.

2 tbs. butter
1 clove garlic, minced
1 onion, finely chopped
½ cup crumbled Gorgonzola cheese
2 cups ricotta cheese
½ cup shredded Parmesan cheese
1 tbs. dried basil

1 tsp. ground fennel seeds
1 tsp. nutmeg
1 cup chopped toasted walnuts
1 pkg. (1 lb.) phyllo dough, thawed
    if frozen
Clarified Butter, page 139

Heat oven to 375°. In a skillet, melt 2 tbs. butter over medium heat and sauté garlic and onion until tender. Remove skillet from heat and mix with cheeses, basil, fennel seeds, nutmeg and walnuts. Place 1 sheet of the phyllo on a work surface and brush with *Clarified Butter*. Cut phyllo lengthwise into 3 strips, fold each strip in half lengthwise and brush again with butter. Place a spoonful of cheese mixture in the top corner of each strip and fold like a flag, until a triangular bundle is formed. Brush outside of triangles with butter and place on a rimmed baking sheet. Repeat with remaining ingredients. Bake triangles for 15 to 20 minutes or until golden brown. Serve warm.

GREEK SPINACH AND CHEESE PACKETS (SPANAKOPITA)

This recipe can be used as a luncheon entrée by making the pastries considerably larger. These can be frozen and brought out as needed when drop-in guests arrive. Thaw for 15 to 20 minutes before baking (you may also need to bake them for a little longer). To keep phyllo from drying out while working, cover it with a slightly damp cloth.

2 tbs. butter
½ medium onion, chopped
1 pkg. (10 oz.) frozen chopped spinach,
    thawed, squeezed very dry
½ tsp. nutmeg
salt and pepper to taste
½ lb. ricotta cheese
2 eggs, beaten
½ pkg. (1 lb. pkg.) phyllo dough,
    thawed if frozen
Clarified Butter, follows

Heat oven to 425°. In a skillet, melt 2 tbs. butter over medium heat and sauté onion until tender. Remove skillet from heat and add spinach, nutmeg, salt, pepper, ricotta and eggs; mix well and cool to room temperature. Place 1 sheet of the phyllo on a work surface and brush with *Clarified Butter*. Cut phyllo lengthwise into 3 strips. Place a heaping teaspoonful of spinach mixture in the top corner of each strip and fold like a flag, until a triangular bundle is formed. Brush outside of triangles with butter and place on a rimmed baking sheet. Repeat with remaining ingredients. Bake triangles for about 15 minutes or until golden brown. Serve warm.

CLARIFIED BUTTER
Makes 6 ounces

To "clarify" butter means to melt it and separate the milk solids from the golden, liquid butterfat. This allows the butter to withstand higher cooking temperatures without burning.

½ lb. unsalted butter

In a heavy saucepan, melt butter very slowly over low heat until the milk solids separate and sink to the bottom. Skim the foam that rises to the top and discard. Very carefully pour off just the golden liquid.

SPINACH AND WALNUT TRIANGLES

Spinach, Swiss cheese and walnuts make a delightful filling that is encased in flaky pastry. There are about 30 sheets of phyllo in a package; wrap the remaining sheets well and return them to the refrigerator or freezer.

1 pkg. (10 oz.) chopped frozen spinach,
   thawed, squeezed very dry
1 cup shredded Swiss cheese
1 cup chopped toasted walnuts
2 tsp. Dijon mustard

salt and pepper to taste
18 sheets phyllo dough, thawed if
   frozen
Clarified Butter, page 139

Heat oven to 375°. In a bowl, mix spinach, cheese, walnuts, mustard, salt and pepper until well mixed. Cover unused phyllo with a slightly damp cloth while working to keep it from drying out. Place 1 sheet of the phyllo on a work surface and brush with *Clarified Butter*. Cut phyllo crosswise into 3 strips, fold each strip in half lengthwise and brush again with butter. Place a heaping teaspoonful of spinach mixture in the top corner of each strip and fold like a flag, until a triangular bundle is formed. Brush outside of triangles with butter and place on a rimmed baking sheet. Repeat with remaining ingredients. Bake triangles for 15 to 20 minutes or until golden brown. Serve warm.

MIDDLE EASTERN VEGETABLE PACKETS

This vegetarian appetizer is surrounded by flaky pastry. It can be made ahead of time and kept frozen until ready to bake; thaw before baking. Keep phyllo covered with a slightly damp cloth while working to prevent it from drying out.

2 tbs. butter
½ medium onion, diced
⅓ lb. white or brown mushrooms, diced
1 tbs. chopped fresh cilantro
1 tbs. chopped fresh parsley
1 tsp. ground cumin

½ tsp. salt
¼ tsp. pepper
16 sheets phyllo dough (about ½ pkg.), thawed if frozen
Clarified Butter, page 139

Heat oven to 375°. In a skillet, melt 2 tbs. butter over medium-high heat and sauté onion and mushrooms until limp; cool. Add cilantro, parsley, cumin, salt and pepper to skillet. Taste and adjust seasonings. Place 1 sheet of the phyllo on a work surface and brush with *Clarified Butter*. Cover with a second sheet of phyllo and brush again with butter. Cut buttered phyllo lengthwise into 3 strips. Place about 1 tbs. filling in the center on one end of each strip. Fold sides in over filling and roll up cigar fashion into a tight packet. Brush outside of packets with butter and place on a rimmed baking sheet. Repeat with remaining ingredients. Bake packets for 20 minutes or until golden brown. Serve warm.

GREEK CHEESE PUFFS

These delightful cheese pastries have a slight sweetness. They can be made ahead of time and frozen until ready to bake (thaw before baking). If you cannot find these delicious cheeses at your grocery store, try a Greek deli. Or, use all feta cheese. To keep phyllo from drying out while working, cover it with a slightly damp cloth.

½ lb. feta cheese, crumbled
½ lb. Mizithra cheese, shredded, or
    cream cheese, softened
½ lb. kasseri cheese or Parmesan
    cheese, shredded
½ cup honey

¼ tsp. cinnamon
2 eggs
about 1 pkg. (1 lb.) phyllo dough,
    thawed if frozen
Clarified Butter, page 139

Heat oven to 375°. In a bowl, mix cheeses, honey, cinnamon and eggs until well blended. Place 1 sheet of the phyllo on a work surface and brush with *Clarified Butter*. Cut phyllo crosswise into 3 strips, fold each strip in half lengthwise and brush again with butter. Place a teaspoonful of cheese mixture in the top corner of each strip and fold like a flag, until a triangular bundle is formed. Brush outside of triangles with butter and place on a rimmed baking sheet. Repeat with remaining ingredients. Bake triangles for 12 to 15 minutes or until golden brown. Serve warm.

CRAB IN PHYLLO

*Serve these special appetizers with **Plum Sauce**, page 133, or look for purchased plum sauce in the international section of your grocery store. This recipe can be made ahead of time, frozen and thawed just before baking. Dried-out phyllo can be hard to handle; cover unused phyllo with a slightly damp cloth while working.*

8 oz. cream cheese, softened
4 oz. fresh crabmeat
2 green onions, tops only, finely minced
½ tsp. minced garlic
salt and pepper to taste

few drops Tabasco Sauce
½ pkg. (1 lb. pkg.) phyllo dough,
    thawed if frozen
Clarified Butter, page 139

Heat oven to 350°. In a small bowl, gently mix cream cheese, crabmeat, green onions, garlic, salt, pepper and Tabasco until blended. Place 1 sheet of the phyllo on a work surface and brush with *Clarified Butter*. Cut phyllo lengthwise into 4 strips. Place a teaspoonful of crab mixture in the top corner of each strip and fold like a flag, until a triangular bundle is formed. Brush outside of triangles with butter and place on a rimmed baking sheet. Repeat with remaining ingredients. Bake triangles for 15 to 20 minutes or until golden brown. Serve warm.

CRISPY CRAB ROLLS

Makes 72

This crab-filled flaky pastry has a touch of heat. Make these far ahead of time and bake at the last minute. To keep phyllo sheets from drying out while you are working, cover them with a slightly damp cloth.

4 shallots, minced
¼ cup butter
2 cloves garlic, minced
½ cup chopped fresh parsley
1 tsp. dried dill weed, or more to taste

2 tbs. prepared horseradish
12 oz. crabmeat
about 1 pkg. (1 lb.) phyllo dough,
  thawed if frozen
Clarified Butter, page 139

Heat oven to 350°. In a skillet, sauté shallots in ¼ cup butter until limp; stir in garlic, parsley, dill and horseradish. Remove skillet from heat and stir in crabmeat. Taste and adjust seasonings. Place 1 sheet of the phyllo on a work surface and brush with *Clarified Butter*. Cut buttered phyllo lengthwise into 3 strips. Place about 1 tbs. filling in the center on one end of each strip. Fold sides in over filling and roll up cigar fashion into a tight packet. Brush outside of packets with butter and place on a rimmed baking sheet. Repeat with remaining ingredients. Bake packets for 15 minutes or until golden brown. Serve warm.

CRAB TURNOVERS

Here, puff pastry encases a creamy dill-flavored crab mixture.

¼ cup butter
12 oz. mushrooms, chopped
½ cup chopped green onions
1 tsp. salt
½ tsp. pepper
1 heaping tbs. all-purpose flour
12 oz. crabmeat
¼ cup sour cream

¼ cup chopped fresh parsley
1 tsp. dried dill weed
1 pkg. (10 oz.) frozen chopped spinach, thawed, squeezed very dry
1 pkg. (17¼ oz.) puff pastry sheets, thawed if frozen
1 egg, slightly beaten with 1 pinch salt
2-3 tbs. grated Parmesan cheese

Heat oven to 425°. In a skillet, melt butter over medium-high heat and sauté mushrooms and onions until soft. Add salt, pepper and flour and cook for about 30 seconds. Remove from heat and gently stir in crabmeat, sour cream, parsley and dill. Add spinach, mix well, taste and adjust seasonings. Place puff pastry on a floured work surface and cut into rounds with a 2½- to 3-inch cutter. Brush pastry rounds with egg mixture and place 1 tbs. filling in the center of each round and sprinkle with Parmesan. Fold dough in half and crimp edges with a fork. Brush tops of turnovers with egg and prick with a fork to vent steam. Place on a baking sheet and bake for 30 minutes or until golden brown. Serve warm.

PESTO PARMESAN SWIRLS

These delicious appetizers take just minutes to prepare using purchased pesto and puff pastry. You can even keep them frozen until you're ready to bake (thaw before baking).

12 oz. cream cheese, softened
½ cup grated Parmesan cheese
2 green onions, finely minced
¼ cup purchased pesto
1 pkg. (17¼ oz.) puff pastry sheets, thawed if frozen

With a food processor or blender, process cream cheese, Parmesan, green onions and pesto until well blended. Lay pastry sheets on a work surface and spread with filling, dividing evenly. Roll pastry up tightly, jelly-roll fashion. Wrap rolls with plastic wrap and freeze until ready to bake.

Fifteen minutes before baking, heat oven to 375° and place rolls on the counter to thaw. Cut rolls into ¼-inch rounds. Place rounds on ungreased baking sheets and bake for 10 to 15 minutes until golden brown. Serve warm.

BRIE IN PUFF PASTRY

This recipe's beautiful presentation is made easy by using packaged puff pastry. It should ideally be served with either fruit or crackers.

2 small wheels (2.2 lb. each) Brie
   cheese
1 pkg. (17¼ oz.) puff pastry sheets,
   thawed if frozen

1 egg yolk
1 tbs. cold water
dash salt

Place puff pastry sheets on a work surface. Using the Brie container or Brie wheel as a guide, cut 4 circles from the puff pastry. Sandwich each Brie wheel between 2 rounds of puff pastry. Cut remaining pastry into 1-inch strips and press on sides of Brie. Crimp edges of pastry together so that Brie wheels are completely enclosed. Place pastry-covered wheels on a rimmed baking sheet. In a small bowl, beat egg yolk with water and salt and brush over the top and sides of pastry shell. Cut decorative shapes from any remaining pastry, if desired, and place on top of cheese wheels. Brush again with yolk mixture. Chill until ready to bake.

Just before serving, heat oven to 450°. Bake cheese rounds for 10 minutes. Reduce oven heat to 350° and continue baking for 20 minutes. Pastry should be puffed and golden brown. Cool for at least 15 minutes before serving. Serve warm or at room temperature.

CHICKEN EMPANADAS

This delicious Mexican treat is easy to make when you use purchased puff pastry. If you prefer a spicier mixture, increase the amount of pepper flakes.

⅓ cup raisins
1 cup hot water
3 tbs. vegetable oil
⅔ cup minced onion
1 lb. diced raw chicken
¾ tsp. red pepper flakes, or more to taste
1½ tsp. salt
¼ tsp. cinnamon
1 tsp. ground cumin
2 tbs. butter
2 tbs. flour
1 cup chicken stock
3 tbs. chopped green olives
1 pkg. (17¼ oz.) puff pastry sheets, thawed if frozen
1 egg, beaten
3 tbs. toasted slivered almonds

Soak raisins in hot water until plump, about 30 minutes; drain. In a skillet, heat oil over medium heat and sauté onion until soft. Add chicken, pepper flakes, salt, cinnamon and cumin and sauté for 5 minutes. In a small saucepan, melt butter over medium heat and stir in flour until smooth. Add chicken stock and cook, stirring, until thickened. Add stock mixture to chicken mixture with raisins and green olives, stir well and cool to room temperature.

Heat oven to 375°. Place puff pastry on a floured work surface and roll out until ⅛-inch thick. Cut pastry into rounds with a 3-inch cutter. Place a small amount of filling in the center of each round, dividing evenly. Brush dough edges with water, fold in half to enclose filling and crimp edges with a fork. Place empanadas on a lightly greased baking sheet, brush with egg and sprinkle with toasted almonds. Bake for 20 to 30 minutes or until golden brown. Serve warm.

HONEY LAMB PUFFS

These Middle Eastern delights have a very satisfying, piquant quality.

¼ cup raisins
hot water
¼ cup olive oil
1¾ cups finely chopped onions
1 tbs. minced garlic
1 lb. ground lamb
2 tsp. salt
1½ tsp. pepper

1 tsp. cinnamon
⅛ tsp. cayenne pepper
¼ cup tomato paste
1 cup chopped fresh tomatoes
⅓ cup honey
1 pkg. (17¼ oz.) puff pastry sheets,
   thawed if frozen

Heat oven to 375°. Soak raisins in hot water until plump, about 30 minutes; drain. In a large skillet, heat olive oil over medium heat and sauté onions and garlic until tender. Add lamb, salt, pepper, cinnamon and cayenne and sauté until meat is no longer pink. Add tomato paste, tomatoes, raisins and honey to skillet and simmer for several minutes; taste and adjust seasonings. Cool filling to room temperature. Place pastry on a work surface and cut each sheet into 16 squares. Line miniature muffin tins with pastry squares and place about 2 tsp. filling in each pastry-lined cup. Bake for about 20 minutes or until golden brown. Serve warm or at room temperature.

PUFF PASTRY PORK SWIRLS

Make this very tasty, easy-to-make recipe far in advance and freeze it. It can be made in bulk for large parties.

1 pkg. (17¼ oz.) frozen puff pastry
   sheets, thawed until just pliable
1 lb. ground pork
2 tsp. ground cumin
1 tsp. dried thyme
1 tbs. minced garlic

¼ cup finely chopped green onions
¼ cup finely chopped red bell pepper
   or pimiento
salt and pepper to taste
1 egg, slightly beaten with pinch salt

On a lightly floured work surface, roll pasty until ⅛-inch thick. Cut crosswise into 3-inch-wide strips. Place strips on baking sheets that have been sprayed with cold water and refrigerate. In a bowl, mix pork with remaining ingredients, except egg mixture. Spread pork mixture over pastry strips, dividing evenly. Brush dough edges with water and roll up tightly, jelly roll-fashion. Refrigerate or freeze until ready to bake.

Fifteen minutes before baking, heat oven to 375° and place rolls on the counter to thaw, if necessary. Cut rolls into ½-inch rounds. Place rounds on ungreased baking sheets, brush with egg mixture and bake for about 15 minutes, until golden brown. Serve warm.

SAUSAGE ROLLS

Makes 120

This recipe is perfect for a crowd. Choose a very tasty Italian sausage, since it is the main ingredient. If you prefer a little spice, choose a hot variety of sausage.

1 lb. ground Italian sausage
½ medium onion, chopped
½ tsp. salt
¼ tsp. pepper
1½ tsp. dried basil
1 pkg. (17¼ oz.) puff pastry sheets, thawed if frozen
¼ lb. provolone cheese, shredded

In a skillet over medium-high heat, sauté sausage with onion, salt, pepper and basil until pink color is just gone. On a lightly floured work surface, roll each puff pastry sheet into a 15-inch square and cut in half lengthwise. Divide filling into 4 parts and spread over each pastry sheet. Sprinkle filling with cheese and roll up tightly, jelly roll-fashion. Chill rolls for at least 30 minutes.

Heat oven to 375°. Cut rolls into ½-inch rounds and place on an ungreased baking sheet. Bake for about 15 to 20 minutes, until golden brown. Serve warm.

SAUSAGE IN BRIOCHE

Great for picnics or boating, this is traditionally served on Bibb lettuce and accompanied by gherkin pickles and Dijon mustard. It goes well with soups and salads.

1 pkg. active dry yeast
3 tbs. warm milk
2 tsp. sugar
½ cup butter, cut into pieces
2 cups all-purpose flour
1 tsp. salt

2 eggs
one cooked 6- to 7-inch sausage, about
    2 inches in diameter, ends trimmed
1 egg yolk
1 tsp. water
dash salt

In a food processor workbowl, mix yeast with milk and sugar and let stand for 5 minutes. Add butter, flour, salt and eggs to workbowl and process for 3 minutes. Transfer dough to an oiled bowl and slash top with an X. Cover with plastic wrap and let rise in a warm, draft-free place until doubled in bulk, about 45 minutes.

Heat oven to 400°. Punch down dough and form into a 10-x-8-inch rectangle. Place sausage in middle of dough and encase with dough, crimping dough edges together securely. Transfer dough-encased sausage to a greased baking pan. Mix egg yolk with water and salt and brush over the surface of dough. Bake for 35 minutes, until golden brown. Cool for 10 minutes. Cut into 12 slices.

RUSSIAN MEAT TURNOVERS (PIROSHKI)

This traditional Russian favorite can be made ahead and frozen; thaw frozen pastries before baking. Instead of sandwiches for your next picnic, make extra-large piroshki by cutting large rounds out of the pastry.

1 cup butter, softened
1 cup sour cream
2½ cups all-purpose flour
1 tsp. salt
3 tbs. butter
2 medium onions, finely chopped
1 lb. lean ground beef
2 tbs. sour cream
¼ cup cooked rice
1 tbs. dried dill weed
¼ cup chopped fresh parsley
1 tsp. salt
½ tsp. pepper
2 hard-cooked eggs, chopped
1 egg beaten with 1 tsp. water

In a bowl, mix 1 cup butter with 1 cup sour cream until blended; stir in flour and salt until a smooth dough forms. Form dough into a ball, wrap with plastic wrap and chill for 2 hours.

Heat oven to 400°. In a skillet, heat 3 tbs. butter over medium-high heat and sauté onions until golden brown. Add beef and sauté until meat is no longer pink. Remove skillet from heat and drain off fat. Add remaining ingredients, except beaten egg, to skillet and stir until well mixed; cool to room temperature. On a lightly floured work surface, roll dough out until ⅛-inch thick. Cut dough into rounds with a 3-inch cutter. Place a small amount of filling in the center of each round, dividing evenly. Brush dough edges with water, fold dough in half and crimp edges with a fork. Place turnovers on a lightly greased baking sheet and brush with beaten egg. Bake for 15 to 20 minutes or until golden brown. Serve warm.

BAKED VEGETABLE AND CHICKEN WON TONS Makes 24

Won ton wrappers are fat-free and serve as a good, but less flaky alternative to puff pastry or buttered phyllo. Serve with purchased sweet and sour sauce, plum sauce or even teriyaki sauce.

8 oz. ground chicken or turkey
¼ cup chopped celery
½ cup shredded carrots
1 tbs. dry sherry
2 tsp. grated fresh ginger

1 tbs. soy sauce
2 tsp. cornstarch
⅓ cup purchased plum sauce or
   sweet and sour sauce
24 square won ton wrappers

Heat oven to 375°. In a nonstick skillet over medium-high heat, sauté chicken with celery and carrots for several minutes. Stir in sherry, ginger, soy sauce, cornstarch and plum sauce. Remove skillet from heat and cool filling to room temperature. Place won ton wrappers on a work surface and moisten edges with water. Place a rounded teaspoonful of filling in the center of each wrapper and pinch opposite ends together to seal. Spray a baking sheet with nonstick cooking spray. Place filled won tons on baking sheet and spray won tons lightly with cooking spray. Bake for about 10 minutes or until brown and crisp. Serve warm.

CHINESE PORK DUMPLINGS (POT STICKERS)

These are common "dim sum," the Chinese word for appetizer.

2 tsp. minced fresh ginger
2 green onions, finely minced
6 tbs. cream sherry
1 lb. ground pork
2 tbs. soy sauce
1 tsp. salt
¼ tsp. pepper
1 tsp. sugar

3 tbs. toasted sesame oil
½ cup chopped water chestnuts
1 tbs. chopped fresh cilantro
30 round won ton wrappers
3 tbs. vegetable oil
1 tbs. white vinegar
1 cup water

Soak ginger and green onions in 4 tbs. of the sherry; let stand for 10 minutes and drain. Place mixture in a bowl with pork, soy sauce, salt, pepper, sugar, 1 tbs. of the sesame oil, water chestnuts and cilantro and mix well. Place won ton wrappers on a work surface and moisten edges with water. Place 2 tsp. filling in the center of each wrapper and fold in half. Pleat or crimp edges together. Heat vegetable oil in an extra-large skillet, arrange dumplings in circles, cover and cook over medium heat for 3 minutes. Combine remaining sherry and sesame oil with vinegar and water, add to skillet and cook uncovered until liquid is absorbed.

BLACK-EYED SUSANS

Sweet dates encased in a cheese pastry are a Southern specialty.

1 cup cold butter, cut into small cubes
1 lb. sharp cheddar cheese, shredded
2 cups all-purpose flour
pinch salt
pinch cayenne pepper, or more to taste
1 lb. pitted dates
½ cup sugar

Heat oven to 300°. With a food processor or pastry blender, quickly mix butter, cheese, flour, salt and cayenne until a dough forms. Shape dough into 36 to 48 balls. Press a date into the center of each ball, encasing it entirely with dough. Roll balls in sugar and place on a baking sheet. Bake for about 30 minutes. Cool on a rack.

OLIVE SWIRLS

Here, olives are surrounded by a slightly spicy cheese pastry.

½ cup all-purpose flour
4 oz. cheddar cheese, shredded
3 tbs. butter, cut into pieces
dash Tabasco Sauce
½ cup chopped pimiento-stuffed green olives

With a food processor, process flour, cheese, butter and Tabasco until well mixed. Form dough into a ball and chill for 30 minutes. Roll dough between 2 sheets of waxed paper to a 6-x-10-inch rectangle. Sprinkle entire surface of dough with olives and roll up jelly-roll fashion. Wrap rolled dough with waxed paper and chill for at least 1 hour.

Just before serving, heat oven to 400°. Cut roll into ¼-inch rounds and place rounds on an ungreased baking sheet. Bake for about 15 minutes or until golden brown. Serve warm.

OLIVE PUFFS

Green olives are encased in cheese pastry and served warm. Keep a large quantity of these in the freezer so you won't run out. Thaw them before baking.

2 cups shredded sharp cheddar cheese
½ cup butter, softened
1 cup all-purpose flour
36 pimiento-stuffed green olives

Heat oven to 400°. With a mixer, beat cheese, butter and flour until well mixed. Shape dough into 36 equal-sized balls. Press an olive into the center of each ball, encasing it entirely with dough. Place balls on a baking sheet and bake for 20 minutes or until golden brown.

PARTY MENUS

The following appetizer menu ideas are just suggestions and you certainly don't have to use all of the recipes. When creating your own menus, remember to use a variety of dishes, an assortment of textures, and, if possible, a mixture of hot and cold dishes. It's also nice to provide vegetarian and low-fat selections for your guests and something refreshing and sweet, such as a fresh fruit dish.

ELEGANT APPETIZER BUFFET

Creamy Crab Spread, page 68
Grilled Marinated Shrimp, page 119
Brie in Wine Aspic, page 59
Smoked Salmon Treats, page 92
Spinach and Walnut Triangles, page 140

French Caviar Potatoes, page 103
Bacon-Stuffed Cherry Tomatoes,
   page 78
Spiced Melon Balls, page 16
Curried Cashews, page 19

BABY OR WEDDING SHOWER

Cheesy Crab Toast, page 117
Warm Cheese Wafers, page 101
Fruit Kabobs, page 98
*Date Bread with Pineapple Cream
   Cheese*, page 88

Lattice Cream Cheese Mold, page 62
Olive Crostini Spread, page 46
Miniature French Quiches, page 104
Sweet and Sour Pupus, page 135
Caramelized Nuts, page 18

INTERNATIONALLY INSPIRED APPETIZER PARTY

Chinese Pork Dumplings (Pot Stickers), page 157

Sardine and Pepper Spread, page 71

Teriyaki Chicken Wings, page 126

Honey Lamb Puffs, page 152

Quesadillas, page 107

Greek Spinach and Cheese Packets (Spanakopita), page 138

Chicken Empanadas, page 148

Italian-Style Meatballs, page 131

Hawaiian-Style Stuffed Mushrooms, page 115

FESTIVE PICNIC

Smoked Salmon Rolls, page 91

Blue Cheesecake, page 56

Eggplant Caviar, page 50

Sausage in Brioche, page 153

Pasta Shells Filled with Shrimp and Vegetables, page 96

Russian Meat Turnovers (Piroshki), page 150

Vegetable Antipasto (Giardinera), page 10

Sweet Pepper Antipasto (Peperonata), page 48

Marinated Goat Cheese, page 17

BIG GAME PARTY

Barbecue Chicken Wings, page 127

Sweet and Sour Meatballs, page 130

Smoked Turkey Rolls, page 89

Hoisin Spareribs, page 134

Herbed Mushroom Caps, page 111

Crunchy Ham and Cheese Ball, page 61

Guacamole, page 28

Clam Dip, page 34

HOLIDAY CELEBRATION

VEGETARIAN DELIGHT

LOW-FAT APPETIZER PARTY

COCKTAIL PARTY
Bacon-Wrapped Scallops with Bèarnaise, page 120
Pesto Parmesan Swirls, page 146
Goat Cheese, Pesto and Sun-Dried Tomato Terrine, page 57
Cucumber-Herb Canapes, page 82
Teriyaki Mixed Nuts, page 20
Cheese Straws, page 22
Middle Eastern Vegetable Packets, page 141
Sesame Walnut Chicken Strips, page 124
Creamy Stuffed Dates, page 99
Brie in Puff Pastry, page 147

MAKE-AHEAD APPETIZER PARTY
Marinated Blue Onions, page 14
Anchovy Butter Rounds, page 93
Vegetable-Stuffed Brie, page 60
Mango Chutney Mold, page 51
Sweet and Hot Date Walnut Wafers, page 23
Paté with Asparagus, page 66
Marinated Olives, page 8
Apricot Spread, page 44

TEA PARTY

Strawberries Stuffed with Orange Cream Cheese, page 97
Pumpkin Tea Sandwiches, page 86
Marbleized Tea Eggs, page 80
Cucumber Mint Coolers, page 83
Olive Puffs, page 160
Shrimp Salad Puffs, page 94
Crab Fondue, page 41
Roquefort Mousse, page 55
Three Cheese Phyllo with Walnuts, page 137

LIGHT BRUNCH

Shrimp Tartlets, page 106
Sausage Rolls, page 152
Crab Turnovers, page 145
Red Onion Focaccia, page 108
Greek Cheese Puffs, page 142
Olive Spread (Tapenade), page 45
Creamy Avocado Veggie Dip, page 29
Pear and Cucumber Tea Sandwiches, page 84
Chocolate Amaretto Fondue, page 42

INDEX

Serve creative, easy, nutritious meals with nitty gritty® cookbooks

Wraps and Roll-Ups
Easy Vegetarian Cooking
Party Fare: Irresistible Nibbles
   for Every Occasion
Cappuccino/Espresso: The Book of
   Beverages
Fresh Vegetables
Cooking with Fresh Herbs
Cooking with Chile Peppers
The Dehydrator Cookbook
Recipes for the Pressure Cooker
Beer and Good Food
Unbeatable Chicken Recipes
Gourmet Gifts
From Freezer, 'Fridge and Pantry
Edible Pockets for Every Meal
Oven and Rotisserie Roasting
Risottos, Paellas and Other Rice
   Specialties
Muffins, Nut Breads and More
Healthy Snacks for Kids
100 Dynamite Desserts
Recipes for Yogurt Cheese
Sautés
Cooking in Porcelain

Casseroles
The Toaster Oven Cookbook
Skewer Cooking on the Grill
Creative Mexican Cooking
Marinades
No Salt, No Sugar, No Fat Cookbook
Quick and Easy Pasta Recipes
Cooking in Clay
Deep Fried Indulgences
The Garlic Cookbook
From Your Ice Cream Maker
The Best Pizza is Made at Home
The Best Bagels are Made at Home
Convection Oven Cookery
The Steamer Cookbook
The Pasta Machine Cookbook
The Versatile Rice Cooker
The Bread Machine Cookbook
The Bread Machine Cookbook II
The Bread Machine Cookbook III
The Bread Machine Cookbook IV:
   Whole Grains & Natural Sugars
The Bread Machine Cookbook V:
   *Favorite Recipes from 100
   Kitchens*

The Bread Machine Cookbook VI:
   *Hand-Shaped Breads from the
   Dough Cycle*
Worldwide Sourdoughs from Your
   Bread Machine
Entrées from Your Bread Machine
The New Blender Book
The Sandwich Maker Cookbook
Waffles
The Coffee Book
The Juicer Book I and II
Bread Baking
The 9 x 13 Pan Cookbook
Recipes for the Loaf Pan
Low Fat American Favorites
Healthy Cooking on the Run
Favorite Seafood Recipes
New International Fondue Cookbook
Favorite Cookie Recipes
Cooking for 1 or 2
The Well Dressed Potato
Extra-Special Crockery Pot Recipes
Slow Cooking
The Wok

**For a free catalog, write or call: Bristol Publishing Enterprises, Inc.
P.O. Box 1737, San Leandro, CA 94577 (800) 346-4889**